INSIDE
SCARS

INSIDE SCARS

Incest Recovery as told by a survivor and her therapist

by
Sheila Sisk

and

Charlotte Foster Hoffman

Illustrated by
Charlotte Foster Hoffman

Pandora Press
P.O. Box 5723
Gainesville, Fl. 32602

The names of certain persons mentioned in this book have been changed to protect the privacy of the individuals involved.

Library of Congress Cataloging in Publication Data

Sisk, Sheila L. and Hoffman, Charlotte Foster
Inside Scars: Incest Recovery As Told By A Survivor And Her Therapist
1. Child Abuse - biography
2. Incest - biography
3. Victims of Crime - biography
4. Women's Issues - biography
5. Sexual Abuse - biography
6. Therapy - with incest victims
I. Title
87-62-448
ISBN 0-9619059-0-5 soft cover

Dedication

My contribution to this book is dedicated to the God of my faith, my source of never-ending inspiration. It is also dedicated to my father. This may seem conflicting in a book about father-daughter incest, a crime perpetrated by males in a society where women and children have long been treated as second-class citizens. I am fortunate, however, to have a father who is honorable, respectful and nurturing towards his daughters and I am truly grateful. He has also been a constant source of support, encouragement and enthusiasm for this book, and for this reason I dedicate my part in it to him.

Charlotte Foster Hoffman

Acknowledgements

To all of those who believed in me and gave support and encouragement when my journey was so painful, let this book forever be a reminder that recovery and change is indeed possible. Your support, no matter how small, contributed in some way to the health and happiness of my girls and me. Please know also that your support has not been limited to just the effect on our lives, but also to all whom we touch and are able to support because of your caring. Thank you.

Sheila Sisk

Preface

Friends sometimes ask, "When will you be finished talking about the abuse you experienced?" My feeling? Probably never. It is not important that I recall every detail, but it is important to me that I say out loud every detail that I do remember. Somehow it gives validation to the recovered memory that for so long had been denied. And recollection IS recovery. I know I will never be finished talking until I have no more memories to recall. But I doubt that that will ever happen. I also believe that I will continue to write. Writing, like talking, is just one more way of accepting, even though it hurts, the reality of my incest.

I spent all my childhood years saturated in the pain of my incest. I want never to be alone with it again.

Sheila Sisk

Preface

Incest is a problem of alarming proportions in our society. A study by the Minnesota Dept. of Corrections, "Preventing Sexual Abuse of Person's With Disabilities" (St. Paul, Mn., 1983), estimates that incest, the sexual abuse of a family member, occurs in fourteen percent of all families. The offender may be father, stepfather, brother, uncle, mom's boyfriend or any other male in the family. It makes no difference. The effects are still the same - deep and lasting humiliation, shame and pain. And in many cases the pain gets buried under years of silence, for the victim often remains silent, fearing denial and rejection if the secret gets out.

Our society is at long last embarking on an era when women can speak out about this terrifying crime against their body, mind and soul. And they are speaking out loud and clear. While this is the most important first step towards their recovery, it is not enough. They must fully recover from their horrifying experience. Recovery is slow, uneven and difficult, but it is possible. Women need no longer carry the burden of their past to their graves. They can heal. They can recover. They can be free.

Charlotte Foster Hoffman

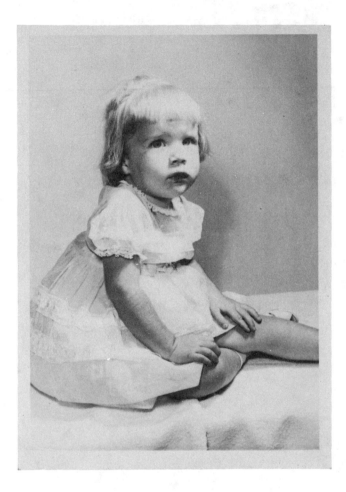

Incestual Lullaby

Rock-a-bye little girl, snug in your
bed,
You can't close your eyes for fear of
your dread.

Rock-a-bye little girl, don't think
you're bad.
It's not all your fault, but the fault
of your dad,

Rock-a-bye little girl, try not to cry,
or dad, he will beat you, and of you
tell lies.

Rock-a-bye little girl, I know you are
scared,
And wishing more than anything that
somebody cared.

Rock-a-bye little girl, he's leaning
over your bed,
He puts his hands into your clothing,
Yes, this is part of your dread.

Rock-a-bye little girl, you need not
explain,
For I was once a little girl, and I
know well of your pain.

Rock-a-bye little girl, now he is gone,
But sleep very quickly for he won't be gone
long.

TABLE OF CONTENTS

NOTE TO READER: The following
symbol, ――――― ――――――
will appear throughout the book each
time the narrative changes from one
author to the other.

I. INCEST RECOVERY

The writing of this book has not been easy. It has provoked strong emotions and brought up endless issues for me to deal with. I've had to delve deep into my memory, recalling all the fear, pain and guilt of my childhood. It has caused me to honestly face the intensity of my own feelings, enabling me to give words to the pain and lasting effect incest has had on my life.

Much of my motivation for writing this book has stemmed from my strong desire to share any part of my recovery that might facilitate the healing process of another life. The work of healing is painful, scary and for me it has sometimes seemed impossible. But with my strong desire to change and willingness to work, along with the caring, gentle direction of my therapist Charlotte, change in my life has been possible and this book has evolved.

Many times I have combed book stores searching for any book I might find on incest or sexual abuse. I had hoped not only to discover the feelings, thoughts and secrets of other survivors, but whether or not they had struggled through normal, everyday life. At times I felt so discouraged, for although I could find personal accounts of incest and sexual abuse, I could not find anything on recovery. I wasn't sure if the incest survivors I had read about had not struggled daily as I had, or if they had just forgotten how hard it was to work through their pain and become whole.

I noticed that a lot of books were written by therapists or psychiatrists about their clients. But they did not relate the things I wanted so badly to read about. What were their clients' feelings, fears and thoughts? Were there others who ever wanted to die because they hurt so badly and felt so

unworthy of life? Did anyone else ever sit
in a corner wanting to cry like a baby? Was
anyone else trying desperately to be a parent
while at the same time feeling like they
needed one? Was I the only one who cut myself
to punish me for not being who I thought I
should be?   Am I the only one who wakes up
at night in a cold sweat, unable to breathe,
trying to figure out where I am, recalling so
vividly my painful past?

Why do I feel so ugly when people tell
me I'm not? Why do I feel so dirty regard-
less of how many baths I take? Does anyone
else out there want so badly to be held or
touched that they would sleep with someone
they cared nothing about just to be held,
hating themselves later because they felt
like the tramp they had been called as a
child? Could I be the only one who goes into
a restaurant and looks for a corner, just to
feel safe? Am I the only one who hurts yet
can't find the words or the tears to express
it? Is it possible I'm the only one who
hears critical-parent voices so loudly I
can't hear my own thoughts? And am I the
only one who feels so divided inside that I
want to try and I want to quit at the same
time? I'm a mother of two children yet I
sometimes feel like a child myself.

So many unanswered questions... so many
secrets. But with Charlotte's repeated assurance that nothing I could say would push
her away and that anything I had to say was
important, I began telling and continued to
tell the darkest, ugliest, most well-hidden
secrets of my past. And with her support,
respect and admiration I have worked on this
book and continued in therapy, hoping not
only to find peace and tranquility for myself, but to also help ease the torment of
others, like me, suffering from the devastating after-effects of incest.

———————————   ———————————

The after-effects of incest are often so
devastating and emotionally disfiguring it is
difficult for most people to even imagine.
The scars are buried so deeply they can scar-
cely be found, much less treated. And the
survivor is so skilled at keeping her secret
that she often forgets it is even there until
symptoms begin to surface. Low self-esteem,
depression, anxiety, relationship problems,
parenting problems, inability to trust
others, nightmares, flashbacks, continued
abuse, loneliness, suicide attempts and
dependency on alcohol, drugs, food, etc.,
are the daily problems incest survivors
struggle with. But the emotional pain of
their experience is so intensely woven into
the fabric of their very being that it often
takes years for them to recover enough to
bring about even slight changes in their
lives. And often the recovery process can be
almost as devastating as the incest experience itself.

As a therapist, I too saw the need for
a book specifically addressing the issue of
incest recovery. While there are excellent
books finally available on the facts, figures
and patterns of incestuous families, this is
not enough. Incest survivors need more personal information. They need to know how to
get to the other side of their suffering and
what the trip will be like. They need to
know that they CAN get there. And they need
to hear it from other incest survivors.

The intent of this book is to provide
an emotionally detailed and graphically portrayed account of one woman's recovery process. It is certainly not designed to be a
model for treatment, but rather a source of
support and encouragement. It is for survivors who want to hear from someone else who
has jumped out into that frightening void and
made it to the other side.

This book is also designed to provide
support and encouragement for helping professionals involved with incest survivors.

It is for therapists who are trying to make their way through the recovery process along side a survivor, because it is a bumpy road for the therapist as well. I went into this experience with what I thought was sufficient training, education and experience. At the time of this writing I have earned my bachelor's and master's degrees in psychology and my specialist and all-but-dissertation for my PhD in counselor education. My most relevant work experience was as the executive director of a child abuse treatment program in Gainesville, Florida. I saw hundreds of adults abused as children during that time, and learned more about victims of child abuse than I did in all my years of graduate studies. And while my job afforded me the opportunity to attend and present at practically every child abuse conference in North Florida, I still credit my most meaningful training to my wonderful clients.

Sheila was the one client from whom I learned the most. The intensity of her experience necessitated my total involvement and continual learning. I intentionally left myself open for the learning I could receive directly from her - and learn, I did!

As with most incest survivors, secrets, manipulations and double-binds were initially Sheila's main strategies for dealing with the world - and me. And while I usually had the objectivity to see it all happening before me, I did sometimes get pulled into her process. That was where the greatest learning took place for me. I already knew all the facts, figures, percentages and general dynamics and had worked with many incest survivors. But the intensity of Sheila's dynamics caused me to learn even more about the actual interpersonal relationship problems of incest survivors - first hand. It was a real "tip-toe on eggshells" experience to be involved in a therapeutic relationship with her and not get snared in the typical interpersonal dynamics that can go so wrong with a

survivor of incest. I could see clearly how
it would be difficult for an incest survivor
to stay in therapy and how it would be easy
for a therapist to get burned out.

Recovery is a long, slow, uneven process
that takes much perseverence and commitment
on both the part of the survivor and the
therapist. In addition, the therapist must
have specialized training and a high level of
comfort with this subject matter. This book
will share some of the more personal aspects
of Sheila's recovery process as experienced
by both of us. Things tried - successful and
unsuccessful. Hopefully it will benefit survivors and therapists alike involved in the
recovery process.

The rare opportunity to create this book
came to me somewhat serendipitously. Throughout the first several years of therapy with
Sheila she would bring me poems she had
written. I was always moved to tears by the
depth of pain she was able to express. She
clearly was born to write. Often I suggested
that she publish her poems as a collection,
but she didn't seem interested. I thought of
all the survivors who could have found healing power in her words. As time went on however, Sheila continued to write not only
poems, but extensive journal accounts of her
daily struggles just to survive. She also
began making transcripts of our tape-recorded
therapy sessions. She said she wanted to be
able to look back at how unhappy she was and
never forget the hard work it took to change.

One day Sheila phoned and asked if I
would take all of her writings and publish
them for her. What a dilemma! All that val-
uable information - a perfectly recorded account of her life throughout therapy - being
handed over to me to "glue" together with
narrative. I couldn't turn my back and let
this gripping chronolog of her life just get
thrown away. So I counter-offered. I suggested we publish her material together. She
could continue to express her pain in her

beautiful and poignant way and I could offer conceptual overviews and insights she had not yet made. She agreed, and what follows in the rest of this book is the culmination of our efforts.

Sheila confessed to me only recently that her original plans were to neatly hand over her writings to me "to do whatever with" and then kill herself. A year has passed since then and that year has seen Sheila rounding the final bend in her treatment. I will always be thankful for the opportunity to write this book with her, but mostly for the extra year of life it "bought" her - a year that has helped get her to the other side.

It is our hope that this book will offer a better understanding of the pain, intensity, loneliness and seemingly never-endingness of the incest recovery experience. And if our words help make another survivor's journey a little less lonely, less hopeless or less devastating, then our time in writing will have been well worthwhile.

_____   _____

II. WALLS

"My well-hidden past."

My life had become one crisis after
another. Up until three years ago, however,
no one seemed bothered by it but me. Stress
and the isolated, lonely world I lived in had
begun to affect the way in which I cared for
my children. I had tried hard to be a good
parent, but in spite of my efforts, things
seemed to be getting worse. I was yelling at
my girls and trying to make them perfect so I
wouldn't have to hit them. They seemed afraid
of me. When I pulled them close to me to
tell them how sorry I was for hitting them
too hard, they would apologize instead for
"being bad." Their little eyes reflected the
love and forgiveness I always knew would be
there, but I was sure that their memories
were recording all of their pain.

As for me, I remember feeling like a
gross, ugly, fat person. My sleep was often
disrupted by horribly immobilizing nightmares. During the day I had a hard time con-
centrating. My mind flashed frequently to
childhood memories that frightened me; sexual
abuse at the hands of my stepfather, physical
and emotional abuse, blame for the death of
my three-year-old sister, and the repetitious
beatings my mother received from my alcoholic
stepfather. My children, ages five and
twenty-one months at the time, seemed to be
pointing out every visible flaw in my char-
acter.

I felt I was of no value to anyone. I
stayed home most of the time because I felt
extremely inferior around others. I felt
very lonely, and in spite of my childhood
teachings to be tough and strong, I was
beginning to feel incredibly weak and vulnerable. I seldom left my home for fear of
rejection, but I wanted so badly to be
important to someone... anyone.

I wasn't sure how long I could continue

this way. I was starting to feel as though I
was going crazy. The lonely nights and days
grew long. Inside I knew something had to
change, yet I didn't know what, and I feared
that change might leave me in a worse place.
But I was willing to try to change if I could
find just one person who thought I could, and
would be willing to be there for me. I needed
to know that this person wasn't going to help
me begin what I somehow knew would be a hard
process and leave me somewhere in the middle
of it. I knew I couldn't bear one more failure. I was already angry at myself because I
thought I should be a better parent and I
shouldn't need to ask for help with something
that was my responsibility.

As a last effort I went to the community
mental health center in hopes of finding
someone who could help me. I was afraid my
problems were hopeless and I desperately
needed someone to tell me things could at
least get better. My girls deserved to have
a good mom, and if I could change then maybe
I deserved to live a while longer. If I
failed to change I planned to place my girls
up for adoption and kill myself.

The mental health therapist began to
offer me advice as to how I could feel better
about myself and improve my self-esteem. She
suggested that I go on a diet, develop an ex-
ercise program, begin to dress nicely and put
on pretty make-up. In one of my visits, she
gave me an article written by Linda Evans
that read, "New Woman of the Month: What
Makes Linda Evans That (wonderful) Way?"
All through the article the therapist had
under-lined sentences and circled paragraphs.
A few of the smaller titles were, "Everyone
you meet is your mirror, Fake it until you
make it," and "Most of the pain in your life
is a result of giving your power away to
other people." The article was good, but
when the therapist gave it to me with the
underlinings I thought of those commercials
with implications like "wear this cologne and

macho men will seek you out; drink this diet drink and you'll look like this; or, eat this breath mint and people will always want to be close to you." I felt discouraged to have received advice from a therapist through a magazine article.

It seemed to me that how I looked was only a symptom of how I was feeling inside. I was trying to carefully hide behind drab clothing, no make-up and a plain hair style. My extra weight was also a way of hiding. But these were all tangible things that I could have changed if I had chosen to. It was the pain inside I didn't know how to change. My self-esteem wasn't woven in the brightly colored pattern of a stylish dress nor could it come out of a make-up container. It was twisted and mangled around the emotional torture of an incestuous and physically abusive past. I was merely reflecting outwardly what was inside. But I hadn't yet made that connection between my low self-esteem and my abusive past. Through the years I had pushed my past so deep within me that I seldom could remember most of it. The walls I had constructed, both mentally and physically, were to protect and hide something. It was that something that I needed help with.

I remained with this therapist for a total of fourteen sessions. Other than a few insights into what I didn't need help with, I felt as though I hadn't accomplished much. In the last couple of sessions much of the focus was on the previously unannounced subject of the therapist's leaving. At this time she referred me to the AMAC (Adults Molested As Children) group of the local Parents United chapter. I wouldn't go. I was too embarrassed. I didn't want everyone to know those disgusting things about me. I was afraid that someone might ask me if I had tried to stop the sexual abuse, and I didn't want to answer that question - not even to myself.

My therapist also referred me to the Parent Aide Program, a support service for abusive parents. Initially I had been reluctant to call. I wasn't sure what they would do if they knew how much I was struggling to get through each day. The last thing I wanted to risk was losing my children. I had worked too long and hard and I loved my girls too much to have some stranger come in and take them away. I wanted help with my girls, but not to be relieved of them permanently.

It was in February, when I was nearing the end of my therapy at the mental health center, that Marilyn and another counselor from the Parent Aide Program came to my home to meet me and my girls. I was so nervous that I moved busily around the kitchen while Marilyn followed asking me questions. I was careful not to establish eye contact with her for I sensed she could see right through my cleanly dressed children and my organized house, right into my painful insides. I wasn't sure if I could trust her to be that close yet. As Marilyn continued to ask me questions, I noticed the other counselor playing with the girls. I was glad to have the space from watching their every move, even if it meant answering a lot of questions.

Then came the BIG question. "Have you ever been sexually abused?" Marilyn got the eye contact I had so carefully avoided. I felt as if she knew the answer but was just asking the question anyway. "How come everyone always asks that question?" I snapped. At that moment I realized I hadn't avoided answering that question like I had thought I could. Marilyn finished the interview and left, saying she'd get back with me. "Yeah, right!" I thought.

——————— ———————

Marilyn came back from her initial interview with Sheila with tears in her eyes and a heaviness in her heart. I can't remember all the words she used, but I remember her telling me over and over that there was something about Sheila, something different, something "special". She tried to describe that specialness but was never quite sure what it was. She guessed that it was her pain, her suffering, her intense child-like need. Whatever it was, she felt it very deeply.

──────────   ──────────

Much to my suprise Marilyn called and made arrangements to come over again. Over the next couple of weeks she spent quite a bit of time with me, both over the phone and in person. We talked mostly about the girls and what a tough time I was having trying not to take everything they did as a deliberate attempt to make my life more stressful. She told me that anytime I felt as though I was going to lose my temper with them I could call. So I began to do that. I called her often and she would stay on the phone with me until I could regain some control. She seemed so caring and sincere, unlike others who had offered me a few ideas, a lot of opinions and even more unsolicited sympathy. Marilyn extended suggestions and examples supported with empathy. Her caring seemed to stay with me even when she wasn't there.

On one visit Marilyn brought a book to me entitled I NEVER TOLD ANYONE, edited by Ellen Bass and Louise Thornton. It had a black cover with red and white writing. After she left I began to read it. I soon came to realize how appropriate the black cover was, for it hid a lot of ugly pain – the same kind of ugly pain my drab clothing hid. That's what's so awful about sexual abuse. It feels so ugly and degrading. I was too ashamed to let anyone know about it, fearful they would see it as part of me like I did...still do. It definitely wasn't something I should talk about.

As I continued to read I was amazed at what I was reading, for I felt I had already read this book. I began to underline, line after line. I couldn't believe that anyone else had ever experienced what I had. I was also shocked that they would talk about it, more amazed that they would put it on paper. I was suprised to find out that statements such as, "Don't tell anyone," or "You wanted me to do this," and "Who do you think they would believe?" were not at all unusual. It seemed that with each sentence I underlined, a small, sharp, darting pain went stabbing into an already sore place inside.

When Marilyn returned I gave her the book. She thumbed through it and began to ask questions - extremely direct and embarrassingly to the point. Was she just that curious about my grossness or was she trying to provoke me into remembering the past that I had worked so hard to push away and forget? I tried to open up a little but felt very afraid; after all, I wasn't supposed to be talking about family things to outsiders. I knew that rule well. But no one ever told me what to say if someone asked me direct questions, and no one had ever asked me so many questions.

I decided to answer as many questions as I could, but I very quickly became frightened. I couldn't breathe. This was scary but familiar. It had happened repeatedly since I was about nine years old. Every time I was frightened or felt trapped I would panic. Then as a result of my tensed state I would hyperventilate, faint and wake up feeling disoriented. I learned quickly to go off by myself so as not to frighten others. So I left the kitchen table where Marilyn and I had been talking and went to the bedroom. I wanted to be as far away from that book and those questions as I could get. I didn't

want Marilyn to see me that way, but she
followed me. She encouraged me to slow down
my breathing. I knew that was what I needed
to do. She modeled slow, deep breaths, and
as I watched her I gradually calmed down.

"Sheila, you need more help than I know
how to offer. I know someone who I believe
could help you. My supervisor Charlotte has
worked with other incest survivors," Marilyn
said. "I'm not sure if she'll even see you,
but I could call and ask her. Would you at
least be willing to go talk to her? Then you
could decide if you want to continue to see
her. Either way I'm going to still be here
for you."

I felt very hesitant for I was sure that
I had already said too much. Yet there was a
certain puzzling relief with each question
that I had answered. And though part of me
was scared to death to be telling family secrets, another part of me wanted to know more
of my well-hidden past. It seemed that the
more I talked the more I remembered. But I
was also afraid that with the next question
something horrible might come flooding out.

I told Marilyn that I would go and see
this person. Marilyn called her, talked
brielfy, then turned and said "Charlotte has
agreed to see you." I remember feeling relieved that she would see me, like I had just
passed an "O.K." test. But a heavy sick
feeling quickly accompanied the relief. It
was all happening too fast. I had somehow
expected that Charlotte wouldn't want to see
me. Now looking back I think I really did
want to see her, but I was too afraid. The
part of me that was too afraid to see her had
counted on her rejection to resolve my ambivalence. I was feeling chased by my past, and
with the partial disclosure and acknowledgement to Marilyn it seemed to be gaining on
me. I hoped that Charlotte could somehow
tell me how I might either push it away or
confront this horribleness once and for all.

I Feel Guilt

There is a place that feels unsafe
    yet still my mind returns,
To find an answer to a question
    that still I've yet to learn.

The innocence you say is mine,
    I want so bad to claim.
But in order to have room for it,
    I must resolve my blame.

III. A SAFE PLACE

*"I'm here for you.
I'm not going to leave you."*

That afternoon Marilyn drove me to
Charlotte's office. I was explaining to her
all the conditions for my seeing this new
therapist. I wanted her to know that she
would need to stay in the room with me, that
I would leave when I was ready, and would
make no promises to come back. The ride to
the office went incredibly fast, and when the
car stopped in front of the office I wasn't
sure I was going to be able to get out. But
as I felt my body tense and then go numb, I
knew two things; that some part of me had
decided to go in and that I was scared
speechless. As we walked in, I hoped to hear
that Charlotte had changed her mind about
seeing me, or at least needed to leave unex-
pectedly. Instead, she appeared, introduced
herself and directed Marilyn and I into her
office. By this time I was so numbed-out I
could barely speak, so I grabbed the chair
with the closest clear-shot to the door.

———————   ———————

It was March when Sheila and Marilyn
walked into my office. Sheila glanced up at
me, mumbled a hello and quickly found the
nearest seat. With her blue eyes she clung to
Marilyn as if she were her security blanket.
And for the next two hours those same blue
eyes ran a frenzied path between Marilyn's
eyes and a braided key ring she twisted and
wound so tightly around her thumb I thought
her skin would surely burst.
I knew I had a frightened child before
me that needed reassurance, so I began by
laying my cards on the table. I told her
what I knew about her from my discussions
with Marilyn; her abusive behavior towards
her children, her present stressful living
conditions and the sexual, physical and

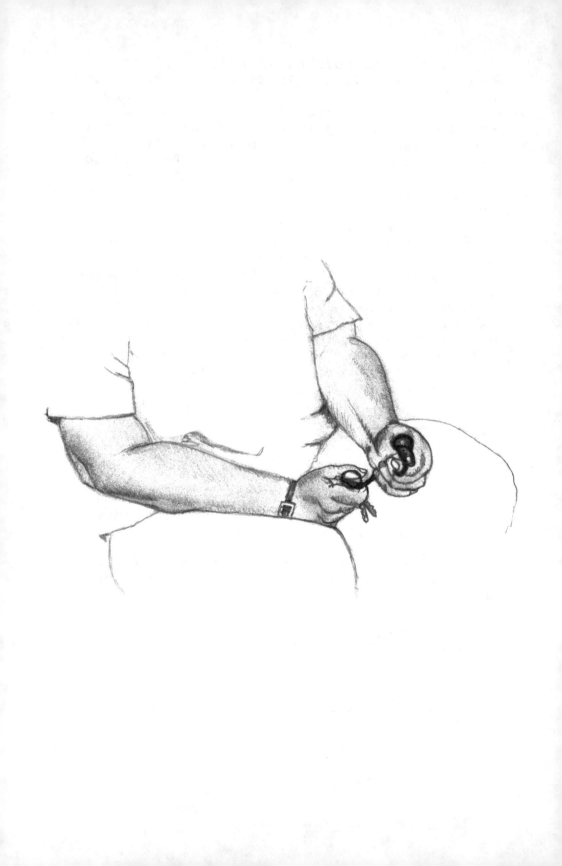

emotional abuse in her own past. I told her
that I knew she was hesitant to talk about
her past - that I understood her reluctance,
and that it was a normal response to a horrible experience. Sheila listened intently.
I suspected she was waiting to see or hear
any hint of weakness or shock in my voice or
demeanor.   I hoped she had not found any.

     I went on to tell her what I knew about
other adult victims of child abuse; that they
have difficulities with self-esteem, trust
and intimate relationships. That most of
them feel truly unworthy, incapable and
unlovable, and that they usually believe
there is something terribly wrong with them.
I wanted Sheila to know that she was not
alone and that she had finally found a place
where she would be understood.

     She continued to listen. I could only
hope I was reaching her. I decided to trans-
late her silence as a signal to continue and
went on to tell her about therapy: that it
was confidential, and no matter what she
said, it stayed only with me. She looked up
at me for the first time and I felt I had
found the key. Now it was time for me to
ever-so-carefully turn the focus to her. But
first I wanted her to feel secure and safe
enough to participate, so I point-blank asked
her what I could do right then to make her
feel safe. "Would you like to move things
around or sit someplace else? What do you
need to feel safe enough to talk?"

-------------   -------------

     I was so busy replaying my escape route
in my head that I had a hard time hearing
what she was saying. But then as if she
could hear what I was thinking she asked,
"How can I help you to feel safe?" My brain
fast-forwarded through all my trapped feelings and I quickly scanned the room.

-------------   -------------

Whatever it took I wanted her to know that I valued her need for safety. Sheila seemed shocked. She was already speechless.

———————   ———————

I looked up for what seemed like the first time, but I still wasn't really looking at Charlotte, rather, looking into her eyes to see where this question had come from. Was it one of those traditional questions that all good therapists should ask, or did she sincerely mean what she was asking? I could hardly believe that she even cared if I felt safe. After all, I assumed that it was my job to make me feel safe. Other therapists had taught me this. But Charlotte's eyes told me she was serious.

———————   ———————

Sheila still didn't say anything, but I noticed she dropped her shoulders a bit and her head tilted a little more towards me. That was all I needed. I knew I was on target.

———————   ———————

I had assumed that Charlotte would be like the other therapists I had seen; walk in and your time begins, and even if there are interruptions, you walk out an hour later. It seemed as if they didn't think about me again until a few minutes before my next appointment. I've had therapists who could not remember what we had talked about from one week to the next. Some therapists had confused me with other clients. Maybe not all therapists are like that, but I don't feel like I'm too important to a therapist if they can't remember what I had worked on the week before. It's also important for me to know that the therapist working with me believes that I can change. Even more important is that they care whether or not I do.

Charlotte continued to talk about her willingness to be there and support me as I worked through anything that would help me to be a better parent. Marilyn gave me a continual supply of supportive glances. Her eyes seemed to say, "I'm here for you. I'm not going to leave you." I listened as Charlotte told me the things she had learned about me from Marilyn. She told me that it was not unusual for someone who had been abused as a child to become abusive with their own children, but that it was not anymore ok for my children to be abused than it was for me to have been abused.

I didn't really think I had come from such an abusive home. After all I didn't have any scars on my body and I had never been taken to the hospital for an injury. I was a difficult kid and I deserved all the beatings I got, and then some. Except for what my stepfather had done to me I thought the way I was treated was normal. I didn't know what to call what he had done because I thought rape was something that was done to women by men they didn't know. I knew this man well, for he had been around since I was a toddler still in diapers. I had never heard the word "incest" and I didn't like the way it sounded now. I had known for a long time that what my stepfather had done to me was wrong because he was so secretive about it. But I figured I deserved that too. Besides, he told me I was flaunting myself and he had to show me what men could do to me. So I must have caused him to molest me.

YOU CALL IT CHILD ABUSE

You call it child abuse,
  She called it spankings.

You call it incest,
  She said, "He hurt me."

You call them sick people,
  She cried, "I love them."

You said she should be taken away,
  She begged pitifully, "Please let me
  stay."

You said, "But they will hurt you."
  Then immediately this response she
  had:
  "Oh no, for tomorrow I will not be
  bad."

     Again, as if Charlotte could hear what I
was thinking, she proceeded to tell me how I
deserved to grow up in a safe, nurturing home
and that the sexual, physical and emotional
abuse I had experienced was not my fault. I
listened attentively but my head wouldn't
accept that. If only Charlotte knew how bad
I was she would think it was my fault, too.
So I set out to prove to her just how much it
was my fault, hoping she could prove to me it
wasn't.

_____   _____

     At the end of the session I told Sheila
that the decision was now hers as to whether
or not she wanted to enter into counseling
with me. She knew I was obligated by Florida
law to report child abuse and neglect and
that I took that obligation seriously. She
knew my philosophies of therapy; that I did

not claim to have any answers, but that I
would help her in any way I could to find the
answers she had inside herself. I had no expectations other than that she spend her time
with me working. Without hesitation she said,
"I'll come back."

———————   ———————

I decided I would come back because no
one had ever seemed so concerned about me.
Charlotte didn't seem uncomfortable with my
disgusting and embarrassing past. She didn't
act like I was a gross person who didn't
deserve to live. She even asked if I was
going to be ok until tomorrow and arranged
for Marilyn to spend some time with me that
evening.

———————   ———————

My first impulse was to let out a huge
sigh of relief and fall back limp in my
chair. Mission accomplished! Instead, after
Marilyn and I shot silent glances of hope to
each other, I calmly asked Sheila if she
would like to return again tomorrow. Again,
without hesitation, she replied, "Yes".
Waiting the traditional week between
therapy appointments seemed far too risky.
I was quite concerned with Sheila's emotional
state and wanted to maintain the momentum and
trust I had worked so hard to build. Marilyn
was also quite concerned with Sheila's ability to care for her children. Sheila had already made many calls to Marilyn at all hours
of the day and night expressing fear that she
was "losing it" with her kids. And the children truly were in dire need of help.
When I first met Hannah she was a bubbly,
chubby, almost-two-year-old who was so cute
she looked like she could charm her way out
of anything. She was still nursing and seemed
to find favor with her mother. Sheila was a
source of comfort and security for her and

she most likely provided the same for her
mommy in return. But I knew this could not
last much longer, as Hannah was quickly ap-
proaching the "terrible two's", the age which
brings most high-functioning, stable mothers
to their knees.

The oldest girl Heather, stole my heart
the moment I laid eyes on her. She was a
frail, anemic-looking five-year-old, with
large, lonely blue eyes. Her face was expres-
sionless and she looked at the floor and
backed away when I tried to talk to her.
But she did not attempt to seek comfort or
protection from her mother. She seemed to
just sink into some make-believe safe place
inside herself. She looked so frightened and
alone. And as I looked at her I suspected
that I was also looking at her mother Sheila,
many years ago.

----------   ----------

Flashbacks

I heard a small child crying, and
immediately I could see flashbacks
of my past and of what had happened
to me.

Then my eyes filled with tears
as I heard her trembling words,
"Please Mom, don't hit me,
I promise I'll be good."

Then I saw the woman drop that
belt, and over beside her child
she knelt.
Now her face too was filled
with fright, as she picked up her
child and held her tight.

And as they sat crying on the floor,
I heard that mom promising to
hit her no more.

But once before I've seen this sight,
another child, she too filled with fright.
But then there wasn't anyone holding that
child, and the other compared to this
seems mild,
(though both I'm sure seem great to each
child).

For by day she was criticized, beaten and
bruised, and at night, quite often,
sexually abused.
And this child I still clearly can see,
for this child, I remember,
twenty years ago was me.

And the child I first spoke of, whom her
mother held tight, was my child and I
both filled with fright.

For I saw what I was doing to my little
one,and realized then a pattern had begun.

One thing that's been quite hard to see,
is my little girls are afraid of me.
So I set out to change, for I refuse to be
another statistic like my mother and me.

Inside Scars

My mom beat me, and though I felt no pain,
the inside scars somehow remain.

She always screamed, and though she isn't
now, I continue to hear her words somehow.

I wanted so badly to please her,
I tried as hard as I could,
but a part of me inside of me
knew I never would.

She was quick to say how bad I was,
how selfish and how hateful,
and after all she'd done for me
I truly was ungrateful.

I'm 26 and still I can see the child in me
still trying to please.
But not just my mom, there are others too
for whom I wait to tell me what to do.

IV. MEMORY

"Pandora's box wrenched open."

Our second therapy session focused on the only incident of incest Sheila had remembered up to that point. It would be another year before she would recall the more brutal and sadistic sexual abuse she had experiened. With great ambivalence and fear she plunged into the dark and icy waters of recalling, detail by detail, the night her stepfather raped her, twice. It was the first time she had ever told anyone.

She began by telling me about a mirror. THE mirror. The one next to the bed. The one that tilted to just the right angle. Just the right angle for her stepfather to view the rape of his own ten-year-old stepdaughter. Just the right angle for Sheila to witness her own rape. Twice in one night.

With every thought she disclosed, a flood of flashbacks poured in and deluged her senses, overpowering her. Instantly she was there again. In the bedroom. In the mirror. Feeling him. Smelling him. Tasting him.

I am just getting home from a school Christmas concert. It is pretty late, around 11:30 p.m., so I creep in quietly so as not to awaken my stepfather. My mom is in the hospital. My stepfather was drinking heavily earlier today, and when I left at 6:30 p.m., he was quite intoxicated and stumbling around. I know the steps of his drunkeness well and assume that by now he is sleeping it off.
He is asleep in a recliner and I'm managing to get all the way into my room without waking him. Then I hear him.

53

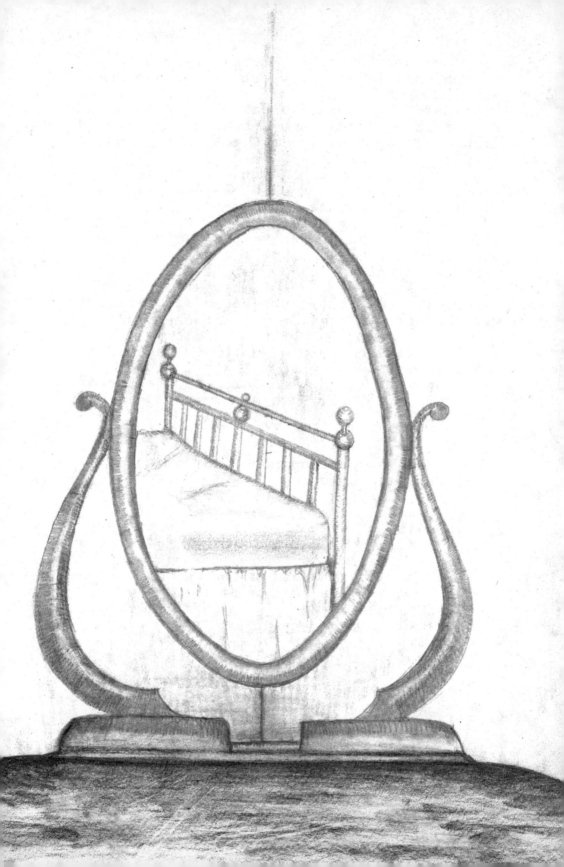

"Sheila.........Sheila.....?
Are you getting ready for bed?"

"Yes."

"After you get ready for bed come
check on the baby to make sure she's
dry."

"O.K."

"Is it time for her medicine?"

"No!"

I'm ready for bed now. I'll lay down
and hope he'll forget what he has asked
me to do or fall back to sleep.

"Sheila......are you coming to check on
the baby?"

I get up and walk to my bedroom door and
stop.

"Sheila.....?"

"What?"

"Come check on the baby."

I walk into the living room where he
had been sleeping. He isn't there.
His bedroom is lit only by the dim light
in the room which enables us to check on
the baby without turning on the overhead
light. I walk to the side of her crib,
but she is sound asleep, so I turn and
quickly walk out.

"Sheila.......?"

"I checked her and she's sleeping."

"Last night you didn't hear her when she

55

woke up and you missed her medicine.
Sleep in here so you can hear her if she
wakes up. You know she could die if you
don't give her her medicine."

I walk back into the room. I stand
there for a moment and then cautiously
lay down. My head is at the foot of the
bed. I'm gripping the edge so as not to
fall off, yet afraid to move further
into the bed. He sits up and pulls me up
to the head of the bed where he is
already laying.

"No. You can lay your head up here on
the pillow and you'll still be able to
hear her if she wakes up."

I feel my body drag across the bed. He
pulls me tightly against his body. I
can smell the stagnant smell of alcohol,
sweat and cigarette breath in my face.
His body is heavy against me. His arms
and hands seem so big as if to totally
engulf me. He squeezes me tightly
against him and moves closer to me....
not closer to me....closer across me!
He begins touching! Touching alot!
Touching all over! Touching...........

---------------   ---------------

     "Sheila...where are you?! Breathe!
You're going to pass out!" She held her
breath and tried to block him from her senses. Her face was red, hot and wrenched with
pain, but she wanted to continue. So for two
hours I sat and watched her take a trip to
hell and back, and all I could do was be
there for her.
     Sheila had kept that secret for fifteen
years and now after finally letting it out,
she found she was unable to stop the flow of
thoughts that came with it. She was shaking
when the session ended and I feared for her

safety. She had already expressed suicidal
thoughts to Marilyn and I feared they might
be realized now.

I was also concerned for the childrens'
safety. With Pandora's box wrenched open and
standing painfully ajar, my fears loomed
large. Sheila and I decided to meet again
the next day with the promise that she would
call Marilyn if the pain became too intense.
I hoped she would make it through the night.

------------   ------------

Silent Cry

Off in a corner, in the darkest night,
  she sits in her silent cry.
Ever so careful, no noise to make,
  for her stepfather waits nearby.

She wants to scream and shout and hit
  and let out loud her cry.
But it's not safe, for still she's aware
  that her stepfather waits nearby.

Then all at once a voice calls out her
  name in the still, quiet night.
And all at once from her head to her toes
  her body quivers in fright.

She hates her name, she hates herself,
  she feels of utter disgust.
But once again she returns to his room
  enslaved to his violent lust.

Trembling and frightened she lay stiff,
  and her body wreaks with pain.
He thinks not of her fear and hurt,
  but of his pleasurable gain.

Then all at once she feels no pain,
  she's numb from her head to her toes;
feeling only disgrace, anger and fear
  as she lay there stripped of her
  clothes.

I went to bed that night thinking about
Sheila. My first inclination was to take
responsibility for the lack of control she
had experienced in my office. Had I prompted
her prematurely to jump into this painful
process? Should I allow it to continue?
Should I stop it? COULD I stop it? Was there
a better, or should I say less painful, way
for her to go about recalling and resolving
her violent past?

I tossed and turned for hours at the
mercy of these questions running rampant in
my mind. Then it finally occurred to me that
I was simply reacting to my feelings of being
incredibly overwhelmed by this person. So in
an attempt to pull myself together, I started
reminding myself that the options available
for resolution of this type of pain were very
limited. Incest victims could choose to deny
their past, but to do so would be self-destructive. Sheila was clearly on this path
of self-destruction. To recollect the past,
however, could also mean destruction, unless
done so with the support of caring people.

The answer then became obvious to me.
Sheila must know exactly what lay before her
and then make an informed choice. And I was
quite sure she would want to continue disclosing her past. For while I saw a shaken
woman leave my office earlier that day, I
also saw her leaving with a sense of relief
in having finally shared her darkest secret.

I had made a commitment to Sheila to be
there for her, and now I was realizing just
how intense and long-term that commitment
could be. I was also realizing that as
painful as the telling of her story would be,
I could not rescue her from it. There was
plenty I could do, though. I could accept
her pain, feel it with her, be there for her,
and in the end, help her find a new
beginning.

*from "Remember"
    by Yarrow Morgan

The memory does not come easy;

it comes with screams that will not stop,

it comes with tears and terror,

it comes with shame that I felt this,

shame that I feel this.

The memory does not come easy;

I tell you because I know,

I tell you because I will not be silent,

I tell you because I will not be

silenced.

*Excerpted from "Remember" by Yarrow
Morgan, in VOICES IN THE NIGHT: WOMEN SPEAK-
ING ABOUT INCEST. Copyright 1982 by Toni A.H.
McNaron & Yarrow Morgan. Cleis Press.
Used with permission.

V. SELF—DESTRUCTION

"I hate me! I want to die!"

I returned to Charlotte for the next
four consecutive days. I continued to make
attempts at retelling, mostly reliving, my
past. The intensity gained quickly and each
session sent me spiraling deeper into the
bottled memories of my past. I didn't understand. Life was supposed to get better once
I had told that dark, ugly secret about my
being an "incest victim." Instead, I was
lonely, hurting and increasingly suicidal.
Each day my energy would be so used up on me
that I had little left over for the girls.
Charlotte knew someone who could care for
them so I let them go. The twelve days they
were gone were almost a blur.

The first night I called Charlotte. I
had been drinking and taking pills that day
and I had decided that things would be better
if I were dead. Charlotte had insisted that
before I made a suicide attempt I was to call
her. So when she answered the phone I informed her that I was "calling." We talked
for quite a while before I agreed to hang up
and let her call Marilyn to come and be with
me. Then Charlotte called back and talked to
me until Marilyn arrived. Marilyn came in,
took a sharp piece of glass that I had wedged
tightly against my wrist, took the phone and
told Charlotte she would stay with me. She
then turned to me and said, "Just one thing
Sheila. Don't you dare kill yourself while
I'm here."

For the following eleven days I played
Russian roulette with my vodka-mixed drinks
and tranquilizers. I didn't want to feel the
pain I had begun to experience. I would
drink and then take pills. When I woke up I
would take more pills and fall back to sleep.
Sometimes when I woke up I would call Marilyn
or Charlotte. I was hurting badly and I
wanted someone to know, maybe even feel, just

how badly I hurt. I didn't want to have to
go through all the pain alone like I had when
I was a child. I don't remember much of what
I said, but I guess I fell back to sleep
talking to them because many times I awoke
with the phone still in my hand. "What if I
had died?" I thought. "YEAH! What if I had
died?" With that thought, I took more pills
and back to sleep I went.

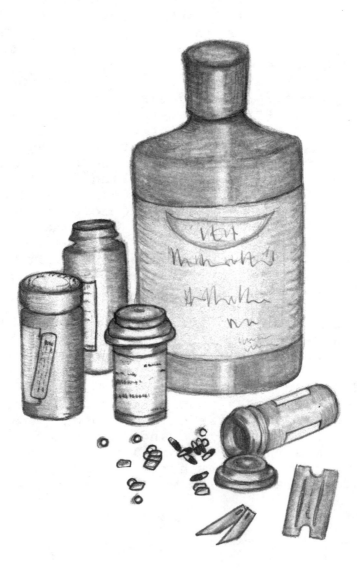

I hate me, I want to die yet there is something inside of me that wont give up, I hate me for that too. I hate me for not trying harder, I hate me for the way I have hurt or entangled others in the life trap in which I too am entangled. I want to quit! I don't want to hurt anymore, yet there's a part of me that wants to continue to hurt me so much that it wont give in to death. But the other part of me will fight it! I'm tired of trying, my life is not worth the effort that so many people have put into it. There is no gain for them and in some cases there may even be loss. Somehow I will push through, for once in my life. I will succeed at what I do best — destroy. And I'll destroy that which is not worth saving and is not PRODUCTIVE —

— ME!

Those twelve days with Sheila were so intense I have difficulty untangling my mind in order to even recall the specific events. Both professionally and emotionally I felt pushed to my limits. I searched and groped for ways to deal with her self-directed anger and pain which were so intense it was frightening. I was scraping the bottom of my emotional barrel for the energy to continue caring for this fragment of a person. And caring was the most vital thing I could offer.

———————   ———————

No more could I block those disgusting memories of my incestuous past. As a child I had been trapped by my alcoholic stepfather. Now I felt trapped by the memories of him. As I relived each horrible, painful moment, they were so vivid I could see them. I remember the odors. I could feel the touches as real as if they were happening right then.

Journal entry:

My memories have hands and eyes.
Large strong gripping hands.
Hands that touch my body.
Hands that hold me down.
Hands that won't go away.
Eyes. Stone cold eyes. Accusing eyes.
Staring eyes. Eyes that can undress me
without even touching me.
Stripped of my clothing by his hands or
his eyes. It makes no difference.
The feelings are the same.
VIOLATION!

I wake up filled with fear from last night's nightmares. I feel discouraged. I think I would rather have stayed awake all night than to have relived the horrible experience of total violation by

him. The nightmares taint my whole day.
I startle easily and feel teary. I feel
sick to my stomach and my heart pounds
heavy in my chest, causing it to hurt.

I stand in front of the mirror, putting on make-up and combing my hair. But
I become afraid when I see his reflection
in the mirror. I turn quickly, but he's
not there. My flashbacks continue to re-
create for me the traumatic events of my
childhood.

I hear a noise in the night and sit
straight up in bed, expecting to see him.
But he's not there. It's only the noise
of my two-year-old as she tosses in her
bed in the other room.

In my room getting dressed, I look
around expecting to see him mysteriously
appear from nowhere, as he had so often
done when I was a child. But he doesn't.
He's not there. But he continues to peer
at me, touch me, and frighten me through
my memories.

For the abuse is still very much
alive and actively destructive within me.
I feel hurt, degraded, humiliated and
gross. And I can't make these feelings
go away.

I searched within myself for some way of
coping with my painful, out-of-control feelings. I was feeling angry at myself for so
many things. For not fighting back when my
stepfather raped me. Why hadn't I told someone sooner? Why didn't I do something about
what was happening? Or had I done something
to cause it to happen?

One day I walked to the kitchen sink and
smashed a couple of glasses. Almost in the
same instant I grabbed some broken glass and
slashed frantically at my wrist. It didn't
hurt, but inside it felt incredibly familiar.
As I gazed at the gaping slashes on the inside of my left arm, my mind flashed to two

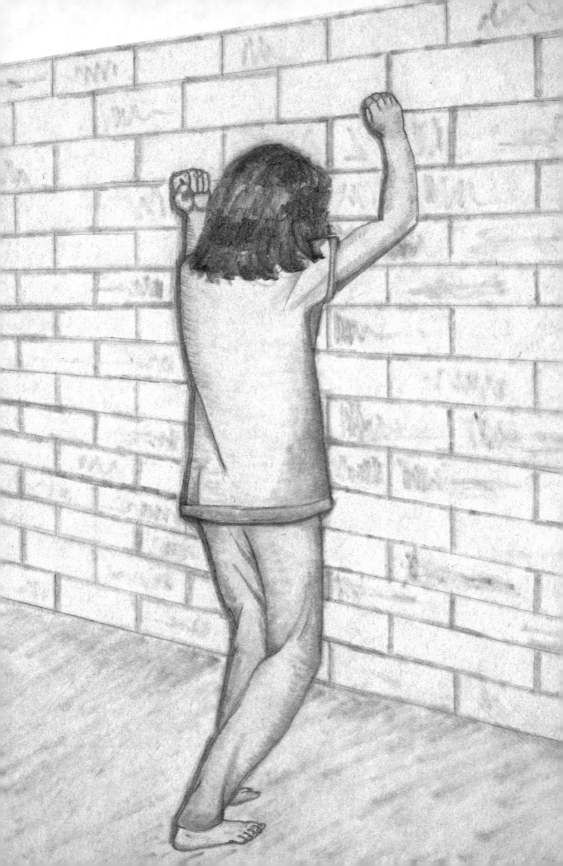

small fists that were scratched, bleeding and badly bruised. I stood there staring at my bloody arm as I recalled one of many incidents where the pain of my abuse seemed so unbearable, and I felt so angry at me for being such a bad person, that I punched a brick wall until I could barely stand up. Tears of exhaustion streamed down my face as I silently screamed "I HATE HIM! I HATE HIM! I HATE ME!! I HATE ME!!!"

That was fifteen years ago. Yet at twenty-six, the cutting seemed to pay the debt and bear up under the pain just as the punching had back then. I had recalled some of my painful past and with it came the same brutal coping that I had needed as a child.

―――――――   ―――――――

Almost every day Marilyn and I would report to each other the drama of the night before with Sheila. Things were going from bad to worse. Sheila was now turning her new-found flood of anger onto herself, too afraid of placing it where it really lie. And we were exhausted! We wanted so much to be there for her and see her through the worst of her pain - to get her over the hump. But to our rapidly growing despair, the hump was nowhere in sight.

Marilyn and I both had a very strong intuitive sense that what Sheila needed more than anything was for someone to be there for her. Not to bail out, or tire out, but to go the distance with her. It's a need we all have. To know, really know, that someone cares enough to be there for you when you can't be there for yourself. To allow you to be weak, vulnerable and dependent. To be mothered. That's what Sheila needed. We knew it and wanted to be there in that way for her. We wanted to do what most professionals are unable to do because of philosophical, policy, or time restraints. We had helped so many adult victims of child abuse

69

in this way and wanted to give the same to Sheila.

But finally we saw ourselves wearing down, becoming exhausted, angry, resentful of the loss of our personal and family time, and fearful of losing our perspective and ultimate purpose for being involved with Sheila. And we saw her needing far more than the two of us could provide. We would have to ask Sheila to use other resources to supplement our help. Although she had made it clear at the outset that she did not trust the community, viewed "them" as the enemy, and viewed us as her last resource, we had to try to convince her to broaden her support network. It seemed like a mission doomed from the start and Marilyn and I suspected Sheila would view this suggestion as rejection, which she did - and in no small way.

——————— ———————

I wasn't the only one overwhelmed. Charlotte and Marilyn had realized that they couldn't continue to keep up this pace. So they sat me down and told me that I would have to start using the Crisis Center for nights and weekends. I figured this was their kind way of telling me that they hadn't realized what they were getting into and I assumed they were bailing out on me. I didn't blame them. I was quite sure they eventually would, yet I had desperately hoped they wouldn't. I listened as they talked. How could I possibly call the Crisis Center to help me through a tough night of nightmares? They wouldn't understand and I'd be too upset to explain what was going on. Besides, they were strangers and often male strangers. I decided "Forget this! I'll bail out too!" I left the room, walked to the back of the office and secretly swallowed forty-five tranquilizers.

——————— ———————

Sheila was unable to tell us just how betrayed, angry and rejected she felt by our
suggestion, but played it out with perfection
several hours later. While I was across town
in the midst of another appointment, I received an emergency phone call from my
office. "CHARLOTTE!!! What do we do now?!
Sheila just overdosed and is lying passed out
on the floor in YOUR OFFICE!!"

ALONE

I'm crying, but no one hears
  although sometimes you'll see some tears.
I'm hurting, but you can't see
  for all my wounds are inside of me.
I'm frightened and not sure how to say,
  but to you I'll look angry and you'll
  feel pushed away.

The next thing I remember was desperately
trying to pull the tubes out of my nose as
doctors were trying to pump my stomach. I remember doing this a couple of times and wanting so badly to die. I woke up later in Intensive Care. Again I felt like a failure for
I couldn't even succeed at killing myself.
    Charlotte and Marilyn came to the hospi-
tal to see me. "We hear you loud and clear."
was their response. They encouraged me to
spend some time on the psychiatric ward.
"It's a safe place where someone will be
there for you around the clock. It's a safe
place to vent your feelings."
    I agreed to go to this "oasis" of a place
where I could have a constant flow of support and a listening ear. Besides, if I decided I didn't like it, I could leave (I was
told by one of my doctors).
    I arrived on the psychiatric ward the
third evening of my hospital stay. I went in

71

the only clothing I had on; a transparent
hospital gown with a hospital robe that left
much to be desired and little to the imagination (patients on the psychiatric ward nor-
mally wear street clothes). The doors and
windows looked as secure as any prison. The
staff seemed cold and unconcerned about anything besides how many hours until they could
leave. They joked constantly about a place
called ITR and another place called Seclusion. I asked another patient what these
places were. ITR turned out to be short for
Intensive Care Restraints and Seclusion was a
room painted puke pink and empty of everything except a mattress on the floor. You
were sent there if you lost control or broke
a rule. And you were stripped to your under-
pants and hospital gown and locked in there
until whoever put you there decided you could
come out.

     I decided that this wasn't the safe
place I had been told. "No Thank You! I
think it's time for me to go home." I went
up to one of the nurses and I told her about
the arrangement the doctor had offered me
about leaving if I decided this wasn't an
"OK" place. She laughed and said "The doctors are gone and won't be back until tomorrow. Talk to them about leaving then!" I
stayed awake all that night . . . waiting.

     The next day I looked eagerly for my
psychiatrist. But when I found him he told
me that if I refused to stay I could be Baker
Acted. When I asked what the Baker Act was,
he explained that it was a court order which
would allow him, as my psychiatrist, to hos-
pitalize me as long as he deemed necessary
for my well-being, or the safety of others.
I cringed. ITR, Seclusion, and now the Baker
Act. My increased vocabulary was scaring the
hell out of me. "OK, I think I'll stay 'voluntarily', but when can I leave?" I asked
fearfully. "If you cooperate by participat-
ing in all the groups and activities and you
can assure us that you are not going to try

to kill yourself, you can leave in a week,"
he said.

My insides sank low. A week seemed like
forever. I thought I would burst into tears
right there in front of him. But I didn't.
I first ran to my room, plunged into my bed,
buried my face in my pillow and then burst
into tears. I felt trapped and alone, and
this dark loneliness seemed to cover me like
the shadow of a large hawk covering a small
field mouse just as it becomes his prey. I
had once again become the prey of loneliness.
Alone can be scary, but the loneliness I experienced as a child was painful.

Journal entry:

Every time I was told "Don't discuss
family problems," I was taught to be
alone with my worries.

Every time I was asked "Can't you do
anything by yourself?" I was taught that
it's wrong to need, even more, to ask for
help.

Then I was told "You can't do anything right!" And with that came a huge,
helpless lonely feeling, for now not only
could I not do anything right, but because I shouldn't ask for help, change
seemed almost impossible. But I continued to try, for the thought of change
being impossible felt overwhelming.

Then when I was beaten and told "You
should feel ashamed for making me leave
marks like that on you!," I was taught
not only to feel ashamed, but that I
should be isolated with my pain and hu-
milation. The marks somehow not only
separated me from the love and caring of
my mom, but apparently were supposed to
make others shame me as well.

Then when I was molested, I was told
"Don't tell or you will be blamed," and I
learned to be alone with my disgrace and

my physical and emotional pain.

I knew every facet of loneliness;
never ask for help, don't talk, don't
trust, don't need, and above all, don't
express any feelings. Now as an adult
I isolate myself physically at times, but
more often emotionally. I push myself to
the point of physical and emotional exhaustion without even being aware of it.
I criticize me for what I can't do, don't
do, and don't do well enough. I moved
away from home and was married at eight-
teen and in just a short time recreated
for myself the same type of environment
in which I grew up - abusive, critical
and one that included much pain. The
marriage ended in divorce. I wished
things had been different, just as I
wished growing up had been different.
Still, I continued to surround myself
with pain and criticism just as my
parents did for me years ago.

I "cooperated and participated" for six
days, during which time I did the best I
could to pretend I could leave if I chose to.
However, I sought out no comfort, listening
ear or support from my male nurse, male doctor or male therapist. I couldn't figure out
why I was the only female patient who was as-
signed all male staff. I guessed it was because I had said that I had come from an incestuous past and was struggling through the
memories of it. I told them I had a hard time
talking about my past but knew it would be
next to impossible with a male therapist. But
when I requested at least a female nurse,
they refused. I trudged through that week
rapidly improving, at least on the outside.
Inside I was afraid because I knew nothing
had changed.

The day of my departure from the psychiatric ward finally arrived. I felt relieved,
afraid, depressed and anxious. Relieved to

finally be out of the locked doors and away
from the threats of ITR and Seclusion. I
felt afraid because inside I knew I still
felt suicidal and saw no immediate resolution. I had gone in depressed and nothing
had changed. And now I was feeling anxious
about what the next days would hold.

   I wasn't sure if Charlotte's caring would
still be there when I got out. I expected
that she would continue to see me because she
said she would. But what would the new limi-
tations she had spoken of entail? And finally, what more would I find out about myself, and at what cost to me and my girls?

———————   ———————

VI. CHANGE — AT WHAT COST?

"Too exhausted to deal with the demands of parenting."

For the next several months Sheila's
therapy sessions centered around one main
theme - regaining and maintaining control of
herself while recalling events and feelings
from her past. Initially, she would begin
talking, then feeling, then hyperventilating
and finally falling out of the chair and onto
the floor in a dead faint. The fainting did
not bother me so much because I knew it was
one sure way to get her breathing normalized.
But the falling out of the chair had me concerned. There was no way my slight, 112-pound
structure could catch the dead weight of her
faint. So, we dispensed with the chairs. We
sat indian-style on the floor and proceeded
to get Sheila in control of her hyperventil-
ation.
      The process took months. Her body would
tense as she relived the horrible events of
her past and she would lock her lips together
so tightly they would turn white. As she
struggled to maintain contact with reality,
she would make an effort to talk to me but
couldn't open her mouth for fear of what
would happen in the flashback she was simul-
taneously reliving. Her chest would tighten
and grow large as she tensed her muscles to
defend against her attacker. Her hands would
be hidden deep in the pockets of her jacket,
heels dug into the floor, and she would back
into the wall to escape the flashback that
was about to overcome her. I spoke to her
loudly, over and over.
      "Sheila . . . breathe! Breathe out!!
Push the air out! Sheila, he's not here ...
breathe!" Step by step she had to learn how
to unfreeze her defended posture. "Open your
mouth . . . look at me . . . stay here with
me. Push the air out . . . not in! Breathe,
or you will faint again!"
      Over and over again we replayed this

scenario. We would both be exhausted when the session was over. But eventually, slowly but surely, Sheila learned to stay focused on me, open her mouth and force her breath out as she talked. She would even call me on the phone, trapped in a flashback, needing to hear my verbal commands to "Breathe!"

The memory came screaming out, so real and so ugly, that she instinctively reacted the way she did as a child; by holding her breath, locking her mouth and calling upon every cell in her body to numb-out to the horror she was experiencing. Her memories were as real as the actual events and her childhood reactions were completely intact. But now, she was learning to recall the memory and react with a new, adult coping method; giving the experience words, making it tangible, making it valid, releasing it.

————————   ————————

Charlotte and Marilyn continued to be supportive in as many ways as they could, yet I felt as though I was continuing to get worse instead of better. With each new-found, painful memory came a flash-flood of anger-laced emotions. Anger towards me and anger towards the girls. Charlotte had tried to point out areas of progress, but so what? I still basically had all the same struggles I had begun with six months ago. Life wasn't changing fast enough for me or my girls. The girls loved me and I loved them, yet this fact made little difference in controlling my anger towards them. I still hit them too hard and too much. I just couldn't seem to help myself. I would lose my temper and hit them or yell at them. Then I would cry and tell them I was sorry and I shouldn't hit them like that. But I couldn't take back the pain and marks of the spankings anymore than I could undo the emotional scars of my unpredictable out-bursts of misdirected anger towards them. I was really starting to be afraid for them.

———————   ———————

    Sheila seemed to be making progress in
therapy. While recalling her past still
brought about, painful physical and emotional
reactions, she was able to get through a session without fainting and was able to dredge
up a considerable amount of details. But the
therapy sessions had mixed value. The release of her hidden past did not automatic-
ally erase the day-to-day problems she had to
cope with. In fact, the therapeutic process
seemed to make life as a mother to her two
girls much worse. Before therapy, the emotional energy that she had used to block out
her past would leave her too exhausted to
deal with the demands of parenting. But now,
with the memories flooding her every waking
moment and invading her sleep, her reserves
were even lower. Her patience and tolerance
for the girls were almost non-existent.
    The telling of her story had to happen.
It was right. But now, it also appeared to
be putting her girls' safety in jeopardy. I
continued to see Sheila's movement toward
health take place at the expense of her
children's survival. And while I knew that
this was only a temporary phase in her recovery, I also knew the girls were at ages
too fragile to "wait it out" or "tough it
out" with her. Their needs were as intense
as hers.
    Sheila was not about to let go of the
children voluntarily. They had become her
reason for living. When the pain overcame
her and thoughts of suicide threatened,
the girls were the only thing that kept her
alive.
    So whose life was I helping or sparing?
The situation became so confusing, so risky,
so dangerous. Up until this point, Sheila
had been just careful enough with her acts
of aggression towards the children to stay on

the right side of the law. My hands were tied. Then one day she slipped. A bruise showed up on Hannah's leg and Sheila acknowledged blame. And while I cried on the inside for Hannah's pain, I was also relieved to finally have some tangible device for relieving Sheila of her parental duties.

Sheila came in for therapy that day. "Sheila, you and I have known for some time that your role as a parent has been getting more and more out of control. I've respected your wishes to keep your girls with you. I understand your need to do so. But things have changed now. You have bruised Hannah. You are no longer able to control your anger with the girls and their safety is at risk. You must place them with someone else for awhile."

"No. I can't! I can handle it." she replied quickly.

"No, you can no longer handle it. Sheila, I have to make a child abuse report, but I'd rather not. Another alternative would be for you to call HRS (Florida State Department of Health and Rehabilitative Services), explain the problem, and voluntarily place your girls in foster care."

"No."

We discussed the matter for an hour. I kept sensing that at the same time Sheila was opposing me, she was also wanting the same thing I wanted. I think she even wanted me to do it for her, but not with the stigma that a child abuse report would bring. More than anything though, I think she wanted to hold onto the hope that things would be different tomorrow. But they wouldn't.

"Sheila, you have until 2:00 this afternoon to meet me back at my office. At that time, I will go with you to HRS to take the girls.

If you are unable to carry this out, I'll have to make a report."

I felt like the village henchman.

———————   ———————

I met Charlotte at her office at 2:00 p.m. with my girls. On the way I had tried to explain to Heather and Hannah what was about to happen. I explained that I loved them more than anybody else in the whole world, but that I had had a lot of bad days and I couldn't keep hitting them. I told them that they would be away from me for a-while, but that they would be back home with me again.

The girls were teary-eyed but didn't really cry. I had managed to fight back my own tears until Heather said, "Mom, its ok. You can hit me. Just don't give us away. I promise I'll be good." Hannah's two-year-old voice added "Me too, mom." I burst into tears. At that moment I just wanted to take both girls and run so I could protect them from this painful separation. All we had in this world was each other and now that too was being ripped apart.

At the same time, I knew they needed more than I was able to give them emotionally and I had to protect them from my anger. In spite of the pain of not having them with me and the pain of seeing them so frightened and alone, there was no other choice.

The girls were in foster care for seven months and that time dragged more slowly than my whole life. I cried a lot and worried constantly about them. Nothing else seemed to matter anymore. I felt like no one could possibly understand how badly I hurt and most didn't care. My total focus became getting my girls home again.

I worked part-time and continued in therapy. Most of my therapy time, however, I spent talking about the injustices of HRS and

the poor care of the girls in the foster
home. I was pretty nontrusting of Charlotte.
I knew she wanted me to take this space and
time just to work on my own problems, but all
I could think of was how badly I wanted my
girls back. I was concerned that if I plunged
into working on the things inside that I
would be even more out of control, possibly
delaying, maybe even preventing the return of
the girls. On the other hand, I knew that if
I didn't convincingly deal with some of my
problems, Charlotte would know I was stuffing
down my feelings and that, too, might prevent
their return. So for the seven months the
girls were gone, I visited with them once a
week for two hours, worked my new job, wrote
continuously, and tip-toed through therapy
hoping to do the right thing.

_____   _____

     Sheila and I both were operating under a
very burdening double bind. Hers centered on
the issue of whether or not to work in therapy. Mine had to with the authority I had
just been handed by HRS over Sheila's case.
Return of the girls would be primarily dependent on my approval and assessment of
Sheila's ability to parent them again. There
were decided advantages to my being in this
position. I was the one helping professional
in the community who knew more about Sheila
than anyone else. And since HRS assumes a
child-protective as opposed to a parent-pro-
tective stance in their cases, my input would
be extremely important as to Sheila's read-
iness. I also wanted to make sure that the
girls would not be returned to Sheila until
she was absolutely ready so that she and her
girls would never have to go through this
trauma again. But I knew my new role in
Sheila's case could potentially cause damage
to the trust I had worked so hard to earn and
that she had worked so hard to accept.

_____   _____

Now, skimming through my journal, I am reminded of the pain, the loneliness and the sense of helplessness I felt and hope never to feel again.

July 25
I can't stop crying. Why can't I pull it together? I miss my girls. Life seems like one hurt after another.

August 1
I'm so tired, physically and emotionally, but I can't fall asleep. I've had about four hours of sleep in the past seventy-two hours. I find myself wandering aimlessly through the house, pausing for a moment in the girls' empty rooms. Even though I know the girls are in foster care, inside I feel like they've died. I feel so alone, so unneeded, so guilty. It's the same kind of emptiness I felt when my sister died. It seems that all I can think about is what I didn't do for them. I hurt.

August 20
I woke up and thought I heard one of the girls calling me, but then realized that they aren't here. Sometimes I sit and think, "I just wish they were here so I could hold them and touch them." Partly just wanting to be able to reach out and touch them and partly just needing to be touched and held back. Sometimes I go for several days without touching anyone, and I start to feel so detached. Like, "Someone, please reach out and touch me, just to let me know you are there, and I'm not all alone with my pain again."

September 10
It's been a couple of months since my girls went into foster care, yet it feels like years. I hurt deeply and feel so alone. I went into Heather's room just

to sit for a moment and reminisce about
the tender moments I had always shared
alone with her. I looked around at her
toys and felt sad. I began to cry, but
my tears quickly turned to anger. I
ripped everything off Heather's walls,
and hurled her toy box, doll beds and
bookshelf into the walls, breaking them.
I swiped off the top of her dresser and
pulled everything from her closet and
stood in the middle of the broken-up mess
and cried. I hated for a moment...I
didn't know who or what, I just felt
angry and hated. I tried to see the room
through my tears, trying to make some
sense as to the origin of my anger. I
could only remember looking up and seeing
some cobwebs between some of her more
readily played with toys, and I felt
sorry and hurting that she was being
denied the right to her room, her home,
her mother, her security. Who cares what
this stuff cost? If Heather wasn't here
to play with them, damn them all!!

I remember my next thought was an overwhelming fear. "Oh God, what have I
done? All this I've done to Heather's
things. Maybe I'm angry at her? Surely
not." As I stood there thinking about
what I had just done, my mind flashed to
Heather's little hurt face. One day I
had told her several times to pick up her
toys. Finally I ran over and picked them
up and threw them in the trash. I had
not intended to throw them away, I was
just angry. She just looked up at me and
began to cry silently. The once smiling
face now distorted. But thanks to my
dares to her crying, there was no sound.
She moved slowly and quietly toward her
room, carefully so as not to exert any
open anger for fear that she would be the
next one thrown.

I finally calmed down a few minutes later
and went to her. I found her crouched in
a corner, sobbing. "Im sorry," was her
quiet reserved response. The guilt went
through me like a cold chill. I grabbed
her up, held her tight and told her it
was not her fault and I was sorry. I
wanted to cry but I couldn't. I felt
angry at me. I told her how bad I was
and I told her to hit me. She said "No
mommy." I told her again in a much
firmer voice and she began to cry. I
hugged her tight as I began to see her as
me when I was about her same age. From
then on I decided that I'd rather die
than to ever put my children through such
hurt and fear as I had remembered growing
up. I never want my children to hurt
like that again

After the thought of Heather's hurt
passed, I still felt angry. I started up
the hall to the kitchen. I felt like I
had to cut myself for what I had just
done. Only that could compensate for the
anger inside of me. I stopped to turn
out the light in Hannah's room and
decided to go in and sit awhile instead.

In Hannah's room her toys were also neat
and dusty. Again I felt angry and her
room was a repeat of Heather's. I sat
and cried and remembered all the close,
cute times Hannah and I had shared. She
had nursed until she was two years old
and then tried frequently after that. I
missed those close times and I hurt so
badly. I just wanted to quit trying. I
picked up one of Hannah's dolls. I could
picture her holding it. I just sat there
and cried and stared for what seemed like
forever.

October 10

I feel pretty depressed today. Seems
like the nightmare of not having my girls
will go on forever. I hurt for what I've
done to them. I think back to a few
times when I felt I had over-spanked
Heather. I lost control. It just seemed
as though my hand that held the paddle
was separate from me and I couldn't stop
hitting. Finally, I took control of my
feet and just walked away. As I'm
writing this I'm remembering Heather's
pained expression. I hurt deeply for
what I did to her.

November 18

Today I picked up the girls for a three-
hour visit. Heather said "Mom, sometimes
when I'm in my bed at night I miss you
and I cry." My heart just throbbed with
pain for her. Immediately I could picture her little face buried in a wet pillow of tears. I too remember that if you
push your face deep enough into your pillow no one can hear you crying.

November 25

I FEEL ANGRY! I FEEL RAGE! I FEEL HATE!
I HATE MY STEPFATHER! I HATE MY MOTHER!
I HATE THEM FOR PUSHING ME TO WHERE I AM!
I HATE! I THINK I NEED TO SCREAM AT THE
TOP OF MY LUNGS "HEY EVERYBODY! I'M
ANGRY AND IF YOU DON'T LIKE IT, TOO DAMN
BAD!"

What is scary is that I have to pick up
the girls in one and a half hours and
somehow by then I have to have suppressed
my anger or gotten enough of it out so
that I won't hurt my girls. I'm tired of
pushing it down. It's like swallowing
back down your own vomit. No one should
have so much control over me that I
should have to do that!

December 5

Today when I picked up the girls I saw
Heather stand off a little, waiting for
her turn to be held. Her face looked
solemn and my mind flashed for a second
to a time when I had found her sitting
off to herself, crying. It finally
clicked as to why I think I keep feeling
so strange about that. It was more than
just the fact that I saw how badly she
was hurting. But it reminded me of myself. She was sitting on the floor by
her bed with her knees pulled up close to
her in a squatting position. I remember
that night with my stepfather. I remember his bed and then I remember being in
the bathroom with the door shut, squatting in a corner on the floor, crying
silently, feeling dirty, and smelling the
disgusting smell of my stepfather all
over me. I wanted so badly to wash myself but I was too afraid he would hear
the water running and ask what I was
doing. I just sat there quietly, hardly
even breathing so as not to make noise
and bring his attention to me again.

December 13

I feel like a lot of people are playing
god with my life. "We'll do this when we
think you are ready. We'll let you visit
the children more when we . . ." Everything is when THEY think it is time. I'm
the only one who really knows what is
going on inside of me.

December 15

I really miss my girls. Today I bought
a couple of Christmas gifts for them.
Somehow it just doesn't seem like it's
so close to Christmas without the girls.

January 10

Last Friday night when I had the girls
overnight, I just wanted to hold them

every minute. They're so cute and
growing so fast. I feel so sorry for
them, especially for Heather. Loud and
clear she says to the world, "Go away!
Do not hurt me anymore." But behind that
pushing away is a little girl like the
one deep inside me, crying out to anyone
who would dare to be there past my anger
and fear. Crying out for compassion,
understanding, healing, refuge, and to be
loved.

It became obvious to me how closely I
identified with my girls. They both looked
very much like me, especially when I was a
child. And because I had become emotionally
and physically abusive with them, their
fearful expressions and withdrawn silent
cries had set a familiar stage for my own
childhood memories.

———————   ———————

VII. DEVELOPING TRUST

"Trying to trust for the first time."

Sheila's determination and single-minded focus finally won out in the end. The girls were returned home, but I feared they had returned to a home not so different from when they had left. For while Sheila remained in therapy during their absence and worked as hard as she could, the work was not fashioned toward growth. Instead, the energy of her work was spent running around and around in circles, creating a dizzying cyclone of anger. Anger towards me, HRS, herself, her family, the foster parents - anyone or anything that got close to her. And her cyclone had built to such force that she sucked in anything that stood in her way, pulled it deep into her center, and frantically fueled herself from it. And her cyclone was very self-destructive, for she was unable to take in any positive input and slow herself down. Instead, everything was used to keep her whirlwind going.

I began feeling helpless and saw my attempts at intervention as futile. I wondered if Sheila would have to twist and spin and rage on until she reached peak velocity, possibly leaving disaster in her wake, until she eventually wore herself down, all of her energy spent, finally subsiding from sheer exhaustion.

Sheila's cyclonic behavior was never more evident than with the issue of her performance agreement with HRS. Her social worker had made a list of expectations for her, to be accomplished before the girls' return. The list included finding and maintaining a job, writing down her short-term goals, visiting the girls on a regularly scheduled basis, staying in therapy, etc... All simple things for Sheila to execute. I've seen plenty of mothers who couldn't come close to accomplishing those tasks. But Sheila was

bright, alert and talented, and the expectations were so far beneath her potential that
to me, they seemed almost insulting. But
that was only my perception.

Sheila saw things differently. She took
the list, the social worker, and the whole
HRS bureaucracy, and sucked them deep inside the cyclone. She became indignant over
being asked to "perform" in order to reclaim
her children, took her social worker's personal style as a direct insult, and challenged the bureaucracy to a show-down on a
multitude of issues. She was unable to stop
the whirlwind long enough to realize that the
expectations were simple and that she need
only to meet them and things would flow
smoothly. We spent session after session
talking about this, but inevitably, me and my
words were also pulled in.

Finally, in spite of herself, Sheila met
the performance standards HRS was looking for
and the girls were returned to her custody.
But the damage done to our therapeutic relationship during that time seemed irrepar-
able. The trust I had worked so hard to
establish had been seriously jeopardized.

Sure, the girls were back with me, but I
was to remain under HRS supervision for six
months. I felt like I was walking on egg
shells trying to look like a perfect parent.
My therapy continued to suffer from the
trauma of the whole foster care issue. I was
afraid Charlotte would reiterate her feelings
of my needing more space from the girls.
True, I could have used more time without the
responsibilities of two children, but I knew
I could take care of them without hitting. I
was also concerned about the care they were
receiving in foster care. Among other problems, my two-year-old had to have her stomach
pumped after accidently ingesting poison.
This happened twice in the first two months

they were gone.

While Charlotte had been concerned for the safety of my children, her primary interest was in me having the freedom and time to take care of my own needs. Once the girls were gone, Charlotte's focus had centered on me and the work I could more readily do when I was alone. I felt so distant from Charlotte during the time the girls were in foster care, and the distance seemed to be growing instead of narrowing now that they were home. I felt like I couldn't talk very openly. Charlotte and I both knew I still had a lot of penned up anger and emotions and many unresolved issues, both past and present. I would come in to therapy unclear about what I needed to work on because I was trying to suppress anything that might threaten my keeping the girls. I still wanted to stay in therapy and continue to work on changing the effects of my abusive past. But I was trying to do the work from the outside so as not to feel or react to the pain. I would tell her I didn't know what I needed to work on but she would say "Sure you do. Why won't you?"

I felt I was working as hard as I could to change, and maintain my responsibilities to the children at the same time. I became frightened, for it seemed as though Charlotte was just an extension of HRS. She knew more about me than anyone. And she had been patient with my outbursts of anger, self-destructiveness and day-to-day struggles with sanity. But I was afraid she would use her knowledge of my emotional state to have the girls taken again.

———————   ———————

As I expected, things had not changed much for the better in the girls' absence. But with our therapeutic relationship in trouble, I felt at a loss as to what to do next. I sat week after week not only watching Sheila struggle, but trying to reestab-

97

lish trust - to get her to believe in my caring once again.

I struggled frequently with the problem of Sheila's great need for trust and dependency and how or where in our society she could be appropriately cared for. Where do people like Sheila go for help when traditional therapy has exhausted itself, no longer works or is inappropriate? Traditional therapy is not set up to mother people like Sheila and virtually re-parent them for the many years it may take before they develop into mature, adult personalities.

I knew full well what the more traditional male-oriented therapy approach would be; to tell Sheila that she had choices to make. Either come to therapy and work or come back when she was ready. Fighting this training was an uphill battle. When I would speak of this case anonymously to other therapists, seeking any suggestions they might have, their usual answers would be very cold and calculated, like "Why are you letting her drain you?," or "It sounds like she needs very firm limits!," or "She sounds like a borderline personality disorder, passive-aggressive, etc. . . ." and on and on. And yes, maybe she was all those things. Maybe not. But so what?

All I could see was a woman who didn't know how to trust. She was abused so severely and so early by the very people who were supposed to have given her a sense of trust in this world. Sure, she could be forced to make a decision. Work or get out. Just make it easy for your therapist.

I couldn't force that choice on Sheila and live with myself. Besides, I really did see that she was doing work. Extremely hard work. She was trying to trust for the first time in her life. And this was going to take a long time. It would take a lot of patience and consistency on my part. Just like raising children, it takes time, consistency and patience to shape them into healthy, happy

adults. And Sheila truly was child-like.
Still so frozen in her childhood. Still
needing to learn to trust before she could
move on to normal adulthood.

———————   ———————

How could I get back to the safe place I
had found with Charlotte before the girls
were in foster care? How could I once again
begin the work that would be painful but my
only possibility for maintaining sanity and
reclaiming the part of me that my abusive
past had laid claim to? I kept trying to
find a way to protect my family unit and get
on with my recovery. I went to therapy, but
the hour would be filled with frustrating
silence while my head replayed everything
Charlotte had ever done that felt
threatening.
     I recalled a time when a pastor had
called her, representing my family's desire
to find out a little about what was going on
with me. Charlotte explained to me that she
was brief and didn't disclose anything. I
got the impression from Charlotte that this
should be acceptable to me, but it wasn't. I
felt like she shouldn't have even given him
confirmation that I was her client.
     Another time the Crisis Center had called
her to discuss my problems with her. They
told her I had told them they could call her.
I hadn't. During this time I was struggling
so much with needing my confidentiality protected that I had everyone take a vow to se-
crecy. Again, I felt like Charlotte shouldn't
have even talked to them about me at all. I
felt she should have asked me first. It did
not matter how little she had disclosed. I
was angry at the Crisis Center for violating
confidentiality by calling and nontrusting of
Charlotte to have talked or even listened to
them.
     To me, protecting my confidentiality
meant not disclosing what I had shared in

confidence but also being unwilling to listen
when others broke confidence. Over-sensi-
tive? Probably. Over-reacting? Debatable.
Without cause for such feelings and reactions? Certainly not, for all my life I had
been violated. I needed it to be different.
Over-reaction is a description used to describe how YOU view my reactions. For me, my
reactions are only a statement, maybe even an
understatement of how I am feeling.

———————   ———————

   Through my years of experience with
Sheila I made a lot of mistakes, but I tried
not to be too proud to acknowledge them and
make amends. I remember one of the most
important things I ever heard my father say
was, "Making a mistake is not such a big
deal. It's what you do about it that
counts." I made my biggest mistake with
confidentiality. That is something that gets
to be a sticky issue in regard to child
abuse. And when state social workers or
suicide issues are involved there is never a
very clear line as to what can be talked
about and what can't.
   Sheila brought my biggest blunder to my
attention several months after its occurance.
I had acknowledged involvement in her case
without a written consent form. And as she
said, it wasn't so much the acknowledgement
that had been confided that upset her, but
the larger issue of trust. And trust was
something Sheila desperately needed above all
else.

———————   ———————

   The recollection of these seemingly small
and relatively unaddressed issues of confidentiality, in addition to the problems provoked by the foster care issues, had begun to
undermine my trust of Charlotte before I was
even aware of it. I had needed to trust her

100

so badly that rather than discussing with her
my feelings of distrust, I did what I always
had before; denied what I felt and pushed the
feelings away. And just as my past had reared
its ugly head, so had the buried feelings of
mistrust. Suppressed feelings don't go away,
they just lie dormant, waiting for a weak moment so they can once again seek freedom. The
mistrust was about to become one of my reasons for leaving therapy with Charlotte.
There were a few more sessions where lack of
openness on my part was made obvious by my
silence. I felt like I just couldn't commun-
icate what I was feeling. Feelings of hopelessness and suicide were again surfacing,
but I didn't want Charlotte to know.

———————   ———————

I continued to watch Sheila grow farther
and farther away from me. The events of the
past ten months had had too much impact on
Sheila for me to work around. I became very
aware of her anger at me and tried desperately to get her to be aware of it, too. I told
her she had a right to those feelings, that I
wasn't perfect, that I could hear her anger
at me without it affecting our relationship,
and that I would still be there for her. I
even went so far as telling her that if I
were her, I'd be angry at me, too. But it
didn't work. She denied the anger and pulled
farther into her fear and distrust.
I think I was working toward something
quite impossible for Sheila at that point in
time...to trust me well enough to be angry at
me. To trust that my response to her anger
would not hurt her even more than she was
already hurting. To trust that I would not
be angry at her in return and destroy her
with my anger. Instead, she chose to take
that anger and place it somewhere safer, more
familiar - on herself.
Cancellations for therapy appointments
became disruptively frequent and the sporadic

sessions she did attend were non-productive.
She would sit, clutching her purse to her
chest as if it were a protective shield,
barely giving me eye contact, and daring me
to ask the question, "What would you like to
work on today?" "I don't know!" she would
snap. "Everything is fine and I can't think
of anything to talk about!"

She sat there looking so needy, so much
in pain and so trapped - trapped in her inability to trust. She looked like a homeless
child looking for a mother. As I sat there
watching her I kept getting this picture in
my mind of her crawling up onto my lap, soak-
ing up all the caring she had missed as a
child and staying there forever. That image
just drained the energy right out of me. And
I was feeling exhausted and angry, too. I had
given to Sheila more than I had given to any
other client I had seen in the past eight
years. I had lost more sleep and put myself
on the line more than I ever wanted to again.
And there she sat, daring me to care and
begging me to care at the same time. It was
a double-bind I didn't have the energy to
work my way out of. I had just given birth
to my third child in four years and was
carrying on with a full-time career. My
husband worked out of town five days a week,
so my family life was quite stressful. I was
exhausted and my health was failing.

One day in a moment of complete desper-
ation, anger and carelessness I blurted out,
"What do you want Sheila, a mother or a
therapist?!" And in that weak moment I lost
her.

------------   ------------

Charlotte's question rang loud in my
head. I didn't answer. I was afraid to because I think I wanted both. And I was confused, too. What was the "therapist" and
what was the "mother"? Apparently Charlotte
saw me wanting both. I felt so distanced by

this question, for at that moment I wasn't
sure if she wanted to be either. I only knew
that I needed to continue to recover from my
incest and change the self-destructive after-
effects. So I knew I needed the objective
direction of a "therapist". At the same time,
I was so afraid and hurting that I needed the
comforting reassurance of hugs, holds and
safe touches that I guessed was the "mother".

I was already feeling suicidal and my
self-destruction was peaking. I cut myself
so often that the previous cuts were reopened
by the repeated cutting. I feared that if I
continued and anyone found out to what extent
I was self-mutilating, I would lose my girls.
Self-destruction had become such an obsession
that I felt like the alcoholic trying to put
herself on "the wagon." I needed help but I
couldn't risk being too open. I didn't trust
Charlotte with this information for I felt
she was already frustrated and angry with me.
So without letting Charlotte or HRS know, I
checked myself into the psych ward again,
this time for twenty-six days. I scheduled
and cancelled appointments with Charlotte
right and left. I was starting to worry, for
while I believed Charlotte still cared about
my continuing to change, I feared that I
wouldn't be able to open up to her like I had
in the past.

While I was still on the psych ward I
requested a pass and went to see Charlotte.
I had planned to tell her that I would be
discontinuing therapy with her. I figured by
now she, too, was probably pretty frustrated
with my repeated cancellations and silent
sessions, and that she could possibly be
contemplating ending therapy with me. No
way! I had to leave her before she left me.
All my life I had watched people who had
claimed to care about me, walk away and leave
me standing alone with my pain. This time I
was going to walk away first. While I knew I
couldn't walk away from my pain like others
had, I could at least walk away from the pain

of having someone else walk away. I didn't
ask Charlotte if she was planning to stop
seeing me because I was too afraid to hear
what I thought her answer would be. So when
I went in to see her, I told her I would be
ending therapy because it no longer seemed
productive. It was hard to say this for
while I was calling "it" (therapy) non-
productive, I knew it had more to do with
"who" instead of "it." And the "who" was me.
I felt sad, for I had grown quite close to
Charlotte.

In spite of the mistrust and distance I
had begun to feel, I knew that for some
strange reason she cared about me and had
always been there whether I trusted her or
not. I'm sure now that if I hadn't believed
that Charlotte was going to be ending with
me, I would never have left therapy with her.
As I walked out I felt so empty. Charlotte
had given me a part of herself in her caring,
empathy and consistency in being there. And
I had just handed it back.

After ending therapy I left the psych
ward. HRS supervision was about to end but
I was required to continue therapy. I decided I would try the AMAC (Adults Molested
As Children) group, hoping that maybe it
would open up another place of support for
me. And I thought maybe I could hear what
others felt and how they were working through
their incest. It seemed like I was tripping
endlessly through mine.

I also began to see Joan, a therapist
who was currently seeing my girls. She was
working closely with me and the girls anyway,
so she agreed to see me individually as well.
She began to teach me how to be nice to myself and give myself space for my needs while
still meeting the needs of the girls.

The ordeal of HRS involvement finally
ended. However, my flashbacks and sense of
hopelessness continued. I was maintaining
only on the continual support and encouragement Joan and AMAC were supplying. Then one

month into therapy she went on a vacation.
However, that vacation turned out to be a
nightmare for her as well as me. Joan had
cancer and wouldn't be returning, I was told
by another client. I refused to hear it. I
had just left therapy with Charlotte to keep
from being left. Now a month later, Joan was
gone and wasn't coming back. For the next
three months neither the girls nor I were in
therapy. I drew upon everything I had learned
from Charlotte and Joan to get through that
time. I was clinging to the hope that Joan
would come back. But she didn't.

   Now I was really in trouble. All the
stress and unresolved feelings of Joan's
unexpected illness along with my already
stressed situation, and I was on my own. I
thought about leaving the rest of my past
buried and trying to just pick up the pieces
and go on. That didn't work. Stuffing no
longer was an option.

   Journal Entry

   When I feel as though I can't handle
   what is coming out, is it indeed what is
   coming out that I can't handle, or is it
   a glimpse of what remains inside, and is
   to come, that is overwhelming? And is
   it my need to stuff my anger back inside that I'm trying to gain control
   over, or is it the glimpse of what
   remains that I'm trying to put a lid on?
   And was the anger that is now unleashed,
   the lid for what is deep (maybe not so
   deep) within?

   I had to find a therapist. I didn't
want to start over with someone who might not
even care if I changed and I knew of only one
person who believed in me enough to help me.
Charlotte. I wasn't even sure if she would
see me. So I struggled for a couple of weeks
with my fear of asking her. Finally I

105

stopped by her office. We talked for a
little while about the past few months. Then
I mustered up the courage for the question I
came to ask. "Charlotte, would you consider
seeing me in therapy again?" She replied a
reassuring "yes" and the child part and adult
part of me sighed deeply. I felt like I was
finally home after a long journey. Back to
where I first experienced caring. Back to
where I had begun to find myself. And back
to where, after years of reaching out, I had
finally found an extended hand.

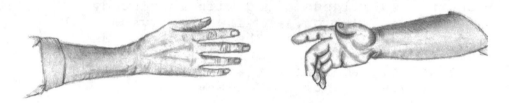

Caution: There's a Child Inside

There is a child inside of me, and though
    she's very small,
There was a time not long ago
    she seemed not there at all.
Then one day I was asked to tell a little
    of my past.
As I spoke and walls came down,
    a little comfort the child had found.
Hiding no longer would keep her content,
    though protecting her had been my intent.
Frantically now she tried to reach out
    to see what this feeling had been all
      about.
For while I was thinking I just couldn't
    cope,
Someone had given the child some hope.
Here began the struggle, you see,
    between this little child and me.
For she had to be quiet and remain
    inside,
    so her guilt and shame I could hide.
Now someone had told her she wasn't to blame;
    and there wasn't a reason for her to feel
    shame.
Even though she still felt guilt and shame,
    she clung to that hope just the same.
I continue to fight her for I feel I must,
    for I see her slowly beginning to trust.
And I don't want her to hurt for I remember
    too well,
Her painful experiences, of which I tell.
But this one who continues to listen to me,
    reaches into the child and tells her
    she's free.

———————   ———————

VII. DIMLY-LIT HALLWAYS AND BEDROOM SCENES

Therapy session: The Crib

During Sheila's absence I took time to recall the events of the past year-and-a-half, and as a result, learned a lot. I realized that it wasn't just Sheila giving mixed messages about needing a mother or a therapist or both or neither. I, too, was confused. I was unsure where one role ended and the other began, or how to blend the roles in a way that was comfortable for me.

All along I had openly acknowleged Sheila's great need for mothering and was glad for the unique opportunity to provide this for her where other professionals could not or would not. And Sheila was certainly acknowledging her need for that. But looking back, in her absence, I began seeing how providing mothering in a therapeutic role was a very tricky task and extremely emotionally draining. And I began to see that understanding Sheila's need to be mothered and talking about it in theory were quite different from providing it in reality.

The alarming truth I finally came face to face with was that I wanted to just be an "objective, professional" therapist, because being a mothering, nurturing therapist was too draining. Yes, I really knew what Sheila needed, but no, I really didn't want to give it to her. And I was angry with myself for not wanting to give it to her. But there I was, face to face with my beliefs - pushed right to the line to carry them out.

And it was hard when it came right down to it because it meant being very emotionally involved, while at the same time having to keep a professional distance - a narrow line to walk, a delicate balance to achieve. To not be too much of a starchy, unemotional, uncaring therapist, but yet be able to be objective enough to not get trapped in the intense, never-ending manipulations.

111

Extremely difficult! It meant being
mothering and caring, but not to the extent
of losing my objectivity.

It seemed the more Sheila dared me to be
a therapist and dared me to be a mother and
pulled herself into a double bind, the more I
felt myself coming face to face with my own
conflict. I was angry to have to come face
to face with such a difficult issue, and
frustrated at my inability to resolve it.

But in Sheila's absence over the summer
I was able to look at my dilemma from a re-
freshing distance. I believed I could be
nurturing and mothering and also remain
objective at the same time. The simple
awareness of the conflict made the difference. I became calmer, stronger and was ready
to offer myself to Sheila in the way I had
planned from the very beginning.

———————   ———————

I was anxious to get back into therapy
because three months on my own had been
pretty frightening. My self-destruction was
on the rise; cutting, drugging and mutilation
of my body in so many ways. Yet there were
so many issues to resolve; Joan's leaving, my
leaving and returning to Charlotte, not to
mention trust issues. I was glad to be back,
but Charlotte and I had to talk about some of
the problems that prefaced my leaving.

Most importantly I needed to resolve my
feelings of mistrust. I felt so wrong for
not trusting Charlotte. After all, she had
repeatedly been there for me. Night and day
she consistently exhibited caring. But trust
had begun, and continues to be, one of the
hardest things I do. All my life I had been
taught not to trust.

The flipside of not trusting is that no
one likes being mistrusted, and that included
Charlotte. She had done everything she could
think of to help me feel safe, but still
watched me continually battle with mistrust.

I remember her once saying to me, "It's been a year and I'm still here and still caring. You ought to be able to trust me by now." What could I say? It made sense that I should trust her. However, my feelings of mistrust, like most of my other feelings, were far from reserved and polite whenever I tried to stuff them. My mistrust challenged everything she said. And I knew if I were to ever get past this, the time was now.

In my first therapy session I decided to tell Charlotte that I was having a hard time trusting her. So I did. "Charlotte, you've broken my right to confidentiality and I'm having a hard time trusting you. Also, it feels risky to be totally honest with you after the foster care issue - especially when you and I both know I'm still struggling."

I had expected her to justify the confidentiality break like others had. The therapist I had seen at the mental health center had given my phone number to a member of the AMAC group without asking and then tried to trick me into signing a release form, after the fact, by saying it was for something else. She got really angry when I questioned her. I had assumed Charlotte would too, for I had never in all my exper- ience with any professional seen one willing to admit a mistake. Usually they not only tried to justify their action, but did so by blaming me for the action they had taken.

Charlotte responded so differently from what I had anticipated that I was left not knowing what to say. Inside I had already prepared a defense speech. I had not expected her to so openly acknowledge having made a mistake. I couldn't believe it! My feelings, for what seemed like the first time, were accurate. I really could trust my feelings.. ....and Charlotte.

That was a major breakthrough for me. I had told her how I felt, she acknowledged my feelings, validated them and extended a promise to be more careful in the future.

113

I could now begin again the work, as scary and painful as I knew it would be, of resolving my abusive past. I needed to trust Charlotte, for I needed her to walk with me, holding my hand down the dimly lit hallways of my life, right into the darkest bedroom scenes of my most painful memories.

_____   _____

Sheila and I were about to walk down some of the scariest corridors imaginable - especially for a child. And as I held her hand through the hallways over the next year-and-a-half, I sensed I was actually holding the hand of a little girl. I silently watched as she fearfully opened locked doors to dark, shadowy rooms, and I provided refuge and light when the darkness began to grab hold of her, letting her know that this time she was not alone.

Many years ago in those dark, shadowy rooms, that same little girl had been forced to endure intolerable pain and humiliation. She was forced to numb her physical senses, stifle her cries of pain and let go of innocence and joy - the very essence of childhood. And now, with great fear and trepidation, she was coming back to reclaim what she could of her lost childhood. Only then could she put together the fragments of her tormented life, find the emotions that had been so void from her adulthood existence, and make sense of the nightmare she had come to know as everyday life.

One of the first doors Sheila opened took her farther back into her incestuous past than she had ever remembered. She had been led there by an eerie and inescapable sound that pervaded her awareness - the sound of a baby walking back and forth on a crib mattress.

_____   _____

I couldn't stop hearing that noise. It got even louder when I tried not to hear it. I heard the crinkling of a plastic mattress and the clunking of the springs beneath it - a double sound. One when a baby's foot went down and another as her foot came up. The mattress and springs creaked and crinkled as the baby walked back and forth in the crib. I felt trapped and frantic. The noise wouldn't go away. I felt afraid for the baby so I tried to stop the noise in my head. But I couldn't. The fear I feared for the baby was all around me... no... rather inside of me.

―――――――   ―――――――

Sheila lived with the relentless noise for weeks, hoping it would go away. But the sound pressed itself into her awareness so persistently that she finally broke down and fearfully began to recall "The Crib".

―――――――   ―――――――

Therapy session: The Crib

S (hesitating) I know there's something about a crib because it keeps coming up in my flashbacks and thinking. It feels significant, big and scary, but I don't know what it is about.

C What are you afraid you are going to find?

S I think I'm afraid because every time I think about the crib I feel trapped and I know I only felt trapped when something bad happened.

C So your worst fear is...?

115

S I'm not wanting to remember anything else.

C What are you afraid you are going to remember?

S Something about the crib is real important or I wouldn't have such a hard time with it.

C So what is it you are afraid you are going to unravel this time?

S Every time I think about it I can see the crib but I can't get past that. Maybe it has something to do with my stepfather.

C Do you hear him when you hear the noises in the crib? What else do you hear?

S I don't know why I heard that.

C But you did. Could it be because it was dark and you could only hear in the dark? Tell me about the noises.

S (hesitating) This is hard.

C What do you hear?

S (long pause) I'm having a hard time.

C Where are you?

S I just hear the noises of, like, a baby walking up and down, pacing up and down the crib, hearing the mattress, the child shift-ing weight...

C What else do you hear?

S (long pause) I know there's something else in the room.

C Where? How close?

S I don't know...I just sense
it..........I feel stupid talking about this.

C I think its very important.

S (fearfully) They're pretty close...in
the crib it feels like...I don't know.

C Don't stop Sheila...."in the crib it
feels like"...

S In the crib it feels like the baby is in
the back....walking back and forth.

C What do you feel at the back?

S Feels trapped....because it feels like
the way out is over the front, but....(long
pause)

C Where are your hands? What do you feel?

S The crib is against the wall and I can
feel the rail against the wall.

C What do you have on? Diapers?

S (angrily) I DON'T KNOW!

C Are you cold, warm? How are you
dressed?

S I WAS WET!

C Was someone going to change you?

S I DON'T KNOW!

C Was HE coming to change you?

S I DON'T REMEMBER THAT PART!

C I think you do. Who usually changed
your diapers?

S   (detached) Different people.

C   Joe ever do it? In the dark?

S   I don't remember.

C   What happened when you got your diapers changed in the dark?

S   (angrily) NOTHING!

C   Go ahead.

S   I DON'T REMEMBER!

C   What do you remember?

S   (almost crying) I just remember trying real hard not to wet my diapers because I didn't want anyone to change me and I didn't want to sleep in the crib and the only reason I had to sleep in the crib was because I wet the bed.

C   What happened when you wet your diapers?

S   Trouble.

C   In what way?

S   It's hard to think about it. I don't know why I wouldn't have wanted him to change me THEN.....I know why NOW I wouldn't want him to change me.

C   Can you remember times when he did change you?

S   I don't remember them specifically...I just remember that he took long to change me.

C   What do you mean?

S   I remember being wet and wanting to be dry but not wanting him to change me.

C   What do you mean by him taking too long?

S   When my sister was changing me I never woke up...but when he changed me........

C   You woke up?

S   Yeah, I woke up!

C   What did you feel like when you woke up?

S   Sometimes,(hesitating)......this time I was awake before he changed me.........I don't know, I just didn't want him to change me!

C   Do you want to stop here or go on?

S   (painfully) I want to keep going.

C   What was it like when you woke up and he was changing you?

S   I was always real cold....

C   Tell me about it.

S   It sounds real stupid.

C   Not to me.

S   I don't know that he did anything.

C   O.K. Tell me what you are remembering. Give it words.

S   (struggling to talk) I just remember that this time I was already awake....I didn't want him to change me... I was cold....my pajamas were already off...I hurt bad, I hurt bad...I was hurting and burning bad...I feel like I'm making this up yet on the inside it feels real.

C   Sheila, how old were you then?

S   Two or three.

C   So you weren't very verbal at that
point. You have an image from when you
weren't very verbal.

S   I remember whining a lot...whining,
fussing, fretting.

C   When he was changing your diapers?

S   He said it was because I wet my
diapers....that I needed to stop wetting my
diaper and then it wouldn't hurt.....but I
only burned and hurt when HE changed me.

C   Do you remember him reaching for you in
the crib?

S   (fearfully) I remember hearing the sound
of the mattress.

C   Then what happened? Did he get a hold
of you?

S   I DON'T REMEMBER! I keep hearing the
crunching sounds of the mattress!

C   And you could feel the coldness of the
wall and the crib and you were wet...

S   ...and cold!...I really felt cold! I
kept trying to figure out where my mother
was. He didn't get my hands. My hands were
on the rail. He grabbed me by the snaps on my
pajamas...I don't remember!

C   Do you want to stop?

S   I don't remember. I don't remember.
The weird feeling is I don't remember where
my mother was. She wasn't in the room. I
don't remember. She wasn't there for some
reason.

C   You want to go on.

S   (wrapping her arms around herself) I'm cold! It's cold in here! I don't know if I just don't want to remember. I just keep remembering a little bit and even if I try to look at it I can't look at it.

C   What keeps you from looking at it? What is in the way?

S   I know I don't want to remember any more.

C   So what happens when you look at it?

S   I keep wanting to say that's all but then I keep seeing more teeny pieces. It keeps having the feeling it's not going to end. It's scary because even though I know now my mom may or may not have been there, THEN I felt like she was protection. A lot of my fright is because she wasn't there.

C   You realize just how vulnerable you were.

S   I felt frightened then because she wasn't there. I remember how frightened I felt then....I don't know...I keep feeling real contradictory.

C   Nothing sounds contradictory you have said so far.

S   My emotions feel all jet-lagged.

C   That was a long time ago. 25 years ago. Those are old memories.

S   Every time I remember something he did to me it feels like there's something I did.

C   What did you do? He molested you when you were still in diapers. What did you do?

S I don't know. I just know that I was
cold and so he put me in bed with him so he
could get me warm ...or so he said. I keep
remembering the size proportion of me to
him....my whole body could disappear against
the size of him. I felt real, real small
next to him.

C You WERE real small next to him.

S (suprised) THAT'S how I knew mom wasn't
there! She wasn't in the bed!

C Tell me about it.

S (hesitating) Just a lot of touching.

C Share it with me. Let me go through it
with you this time.

S (forcing herself to talk) I felt bad for
wetting my pants. I hurt and burn every time
because I wet my pants. That was a time I
didn't feel like I could move any part of me
if he didn't want me to. I don't know what
he was doing, I just know he wouldn't let go
and he held on to me real tight....and
hurting and burning...and it was like I
thought he was going to take me back to bed
with him but we didn't lay this way, we lay
that way.

C Across the bed. It was real different.

S But I don't remember him putting me back
to bed. I know he lay on top of me some
because I remember feeling crushed...feeling
like there was no part of me that would show
from the outside, like if you were looking
down all you could see was him, you couldn't
see me at all. I felt like nothing. I
couldn't even move my FINGER. But I don't
remember his face at my face...his body was
just so big and mine was so little. I feel
almost like it didn't happen because I feel

the feelings but I can't see me...I'm really not here or something. I don't remember going back to my bed, I just remember hurting and burning and not being able to move and no one could find me...I couldn't be found...my mom couldn't find me. I felt like I didn't exist...except for the hurting and burning... like I just WASN'T. I just feel real strange inside...like I wasn't there.

C   Where were you?

S   I was just afraid my mom couldn't find me. I couldn't breathe, I couldn't move. It doesn't feel like the first time either. There are just so many gaps. It's not free-flowing...all broken up.

C   It was 25 years ago....too early to have complete, intact memory.

S   (crying) That time was really scary because I kept trying to reach my hand out to reach my mother, and for a long time I couldn't get my hand out...but then I got my hand out and I reached and she wasn't there, so I put my hand back under because I wanted it to be that she couldn't find me.

C   That's easier to live with.

S   (crying) It was real scary because when I first started reaching out I kept reaching and reaching and I thought I was reaching far enough because she was probably over on the edge...then I remembered we weren't lying on the bed that way. I feel like it was some-body else, but I feel hurt.

C   No it was you...it was you from the very outset...that's the way you remember life from the very beginning ...being on your own and trapped.

S (crying) She always wasn't there.....
wasn't there.

C She abandoned you from the beginning and
that's all you remember...not being protected

S (crying) I start remembering and not
wanting to talk about it because I kept
feeling angry, because if I hadn't wet the
bed and reached out I wouldn't have known she
wasn't there.

C You couldn't take care of yourself back
then....and you were left in an unsafe place.
You didn't do anything. Of course you wet
the bed. Your body was being molested!

S (crying) But he kept telling me I was so
bad because I wet the bed.

C They've made it your problem all through
the years. They've always found some way of
making it your fault. A lot of abused kids
wet the bed. You weren't sent in there
because you were wetting the bed, but you
were wetting the bed because you were being
molested.   I have complete respect for you
that you have survived all these years when
all you've known is abuse of your body. It
all started so early in your life. I have
respect for you that you've survived such a
living hell. You have incredible coping
powers.

S (crying) I remember reaching so far. I
couldn't make my arm go any farther.

C She wasn't there.

S (crying) When I realized she wasn't
there I put my arm back in real quick because
I wanted to some how not believe that she was
not there.

C   Remember that!!   That way back in the
beginning you DID try to escape.   You DID
look for a way out.   And THAT hurt more than
anything else.   And you learned real fast
that it is easier to deal with the pain of
being trapped than with the pain of being
abandoned.   You didn't go along willingly,
you just learned very early that it didn't
make a bit of difference what you did.

IX. REUNITING
FRAGMENTS

Therapy Session: Hands

I felt like the hallway grew longer and
scarier with each step I took. And just
about the time I thought I was rounding a
corner into daylight I'd find myself in another scary room. I'd stand frozen in the
middle of the room as I watched my hurts,
fears and humiliations come leaping out at
me.

Therapy session: Hands

C Sometimes you put your hands underneath you?

S Sometimes I would put my hands
underneath me because if I put my hands out
then he would put his hands across mine just
to pin my hands. It felt safer somehow for
me to make my hands be pinned, because when I
pinned them I could let them go when I wanted
them to. And if they were pinned under me he
wouldn't try to pin me down because they
weren't up there.

C Or?

S Or if they were out there and he didn't
pin them he took them and he would make my
hands do what he wanted.

C He would put your hands on his penis?

S (hesitating) I kept trying to make my
hand not, like...I couldn't pull away. I
wanted to pull away...but I didn't want to
touch it...and I couldn't not touch it,and I
kept trying. And that was another thing. I
couldn't numb-out and I couldn't not feel. I
couldn't, I couldn't, and I would like...be
out of me and not really part of it but my
hands wouldn't leave. My hands still hurt.

C You couldn't numb-out your hands so you were caught there, too. If your hands were under you, you couldn't push him away, and if your hands were out he would make you do disgusting things with them or pin you down.

S Sometimes my hands would just involuntarily go up...especially when I started to go in there or the first time he touched me...before I could numb-out. I would try to numb-out before I went to the room and I couldn't. After the first touch I could numb-out, but at first my hands would go up and whenever they did he would either pin them or use them to do what he wanted. So I tried to pin my hands so he wouldn't do that. Remember that last poem I wrote? I was speaking about the one time I tried to push him away. I didn't want my hand to get caught because I was too afraid he would use my hand so I just tried to make me not do anything with my hand. One hand I pinned under me and one I made fall off the side of the bed. I could feel the side of the bed and I'd know I didn't have my hand up.

C So that was the little girl hand you wrote about.

S It was like, if someone just gave up and died. Like, "I give up, I quit." That hand did. Like, there is nothing I can do. I couldn't win with that hand. If I used it to fight back then it would be worse because he would make me touch him or he would pin it down. And I couldn't make it stay beside me because I wanted...I wanted to push him away. It was almost as if my hand had a mind of its own. In spite of how numb I got, and in spite of how much I kept saying "don't touch, don't breathe, don't push, don't move," it was hard to, because my hand always wanted to be there in between me and him. I wanted something between us, and my hands felt like something I could separate with. And he

130

would take them and use them and then the
separating didn't work any more. And they
were also there because when he wanted to
push me beyond what I could endure, my hands
would act defensively. Like sometimes when I
felt like I was about to lose control or not
be able to not move, I would pin my own hands
underneath so I wouldn't move. Sort of like,
I don't know...I always felt out of control
with my hands.

ONE PAINFUL MEMORY

Today I heard a child cry out so I quickly
turned and looked about.
I saw no child but heard the cry again.
Suddenly I realized it had come from
within.

And as I strained my heart to see,
I saw the little girl in me.
I expected her to run and hide as she
has before when I've looked inside.

She seemed to want to reach out to me,
but instead she watched me cautiously.
And as I looked into her eyes,
my heart began to empathize.

On her cheek I saw a tear,
in her heart I saw her fear.
Then she began to let me see one of her
painful memories.

I tried to look, but then turned away,
as I saw his body on top of her lay.
Looking back I saw tears of disgrace
trickling down the side of her face.

Her small frail hand beside her lay,
wanting to push his body away.
Instead it fell limp off the side of the
bed and again I had to turn my head.

I didn't look back for I could bear no
more,
It seemed as though I'd been there before.

For though I didn't look back again,
If you asked I could tell you how her
memory ends.

My memories were louder and scarier than
I had ever experienced before. I stood in
the middle of my most horrible fears and
experiences, too afraid to scream or move.
And just as my gut was ready to give up and
allow my memories to take possession of my
sanity, I'd feel a startling yet familiar
hand on my shoulder, turning me towards the
door, making this experience different than
before. For now I had a way out and someone
who cared that I was hurting. Charlotte took
my hand and led me back out of the door that
had shut so tightly behind me. Tears
streamed down my face and sound came to my
once silent tears. And as I left that scary
place behind I brought with me one more
fragmented piece of my life that once again
belonged to me.

Sheila's life was a jumbled-up, confusing array of fragments that were scattered
throughout every aspect of her daily life.
And her instinctive urge was to gather as
many of those fragments as possible and fit
them together like pieces of a gigantic jig-
saw puzzle. She wanted to know who she really
was. All of her life she had been someone
else's expectations.

Her personality had become fragmented
from her efforts to cope with her traumatic
past. She was like a collection of many
separate personalities representing different developmental stages of her childhood and
different types of adults. The ones she
brought to therapy most often were the parts
that owned her critical-parent messages and
her frightened-little-girl feelings. She
clearly did not have a multiple personality
disorder, however, and she was quite coherent
and amazingly aware of the transitions from
one aspect of her personality to another.

We talked endlessly about the struggle
between her stifled, tormented little-girl-

self and her perfectionist, compulsive adult-self. The little girl in her was so obviously screaming out to be freed of the horrible secrets she had lived with for so long. She wanted someone to believe her stories, make them real and allow her to express all the feelings that were stifled so long ago. But she was also afraid of the very thing she wanted most to let go of.

Sheila's critical adult-self most often beat down her little-girl-self in the way she had learned from her parents; with shame, disgust, embarrassment and a truckload of "shoulds"; "My little-girl-self should be able to...forget those things...rise above them...stop feeling sorry for herself...leave me alone...stop being such a baby...realize that what happened wasn't such a big deal." And on and on. Encouraging her little-girl-self to talk in therapy and replacing her critical-parent responses with supportive, nurturing messages took Sheila a very long time. But she knew that if she were ever to become a whole person again her fragments would have to be reunited and reintegrated with much love and understanding.

———————   ———————

Torn-------Between

My adult tries hard to understand,
My child screams out in fright.

My adult tries hard to let it go,
My child remembers each night.

My adult wants to take control of
my life and become the best I can be.

My child is trembling and silently
screams, "Won't somebody please
help me?"

My adult looks deep inside herself to
find the child who's crying.

The child expects again to be hurt.
My adult can't find where she's hiding.

My Adult vs. the child

Each night as the adult lays in her bed
    her childhood fears play in her head.

She tries hard to block out fear
    as the child's blue eyes begin to tear.

The child sits up as the adult wants to lay,
    the adult now explaining her fears away.

The child is still frightened yet tries to
    behave, in fear of the adult, as for now,
    she'll obey.

But as the adult begins to rest,
    the child's little mind flashes to the
    molest.

135

The child still trembling now silently
    screams, the adult still sleeping begins
    to dream.

The adult now sees, again the screams she
    can hear. Now she too trembles and
    awakens in fear.

And for awhile they both sit quivering in
    fright, as the child continues to
    experience each night.

But somehow between all the silent screams,
    the adult starts to realize it's only a
    dream.

Yet the child is still screaming for to her
    it is real, though the adult can numb-
    out, the child still can feel.

The adult now stifles the silent screams,
    in order to gain control of her dreams.

The child now looking for someone to hold
    her, finds only the adult ever ready to
    scold her.

X. VALIDATION AND ENCOURAGEMENT

Therapy Session: Gag

Sheila had settled into a regular pattern of weekly therapy and continued recount-
ing incident after incident of horrifying
sexual abuse and mental torment. She had
come so far from two years earlier when she
could barely recall small glimpses of her
childhood without passing out in my office
and frantically turning to suicide to escape
the pain. And while suicidal thoughts still
lurked in her mind, they were gradually being
replaced by feelings of hope and possibility.
She was moving up the continuum, away from
denial, guilt and self-hatred and on to
acceptance, anger and self-respect.

But no matter how much progress she had
made and how much time had lapsed, the inescapable truth was that dredging up memories
of her incestuous past was just downright
painful. Most therapy sessions geared up
with thirty-or-so minutes of courage-build-
ing on Sheila's part. My part was to support
that process. I did so by letting her know,
over and over again, that I believed her
stories, that what she had to say was important, and that no matter how horrible her
past was she couldn't push me away.

I must have said "I believe you" at
least one hundred times and "Tell me more"
just as many. One day I asked her if I was
starting to sound like a broken record. She
adamantly replied "No!" and went on to explain that she could never hear "I believe
you" enough to counteract all the brainwash-
ing she had received as a child that her
stories were just malicious fantasies.

We then had a long discussion about
messages that are essential for incest survivors to receive if they are ever to heal.
The messages that Sheila ranked as most helpful were:

1) I believe you.
2) It wasn't your fault.
3) I'm interested in hearing more.
4) Let me go through it with you this time.
5) Tell me what you're remembering.
6) Give words to your tears.
7) How can I help you feel safe?
8) It's a normal response to a horrible experience.
9) Help me understand.
10) Nothing you can say will push me away.
11) Feelings aren't rational, they just "are".
12) I'd feel angry, too.
13) I'm sure there are secrets you still keep from me, and that's o.k.

Sheila also shared responses she received frequently from others. Some of them were meant to be supportive and caring, but in actuality were discouraging and accusing.

1) Did you try to stop the abuse?
2) Did you provoke it?
3) Did you try to tell someone?
4) Did it happen to anyone else in your family?
5) Why do you think it happened just to you?
6) You can't blame others for your problems all your life.
7) That happened a long time ago. Why are you still talking about it?
8) All of us have had things happen to us but we don't go around talking about them all the time.
9) That's not something I'd go around talking about if I were you.
10) Can't you just forget about it

and get on with your life? Pretend it never happened?
11) (from men) I'm safe. You can
trust me. This is a world full of
men and you can't go around being
afraid of men all your life.
Anything you can tell a woman you
can tell a man. We've heard it
all!

Sheila needed to hear all the encouraging, supportive remarks I could offer during
the next therapy session. She wanted to tell
me about one of the most humiliating experiences she could remember from her past. So
for an hour she sat tight-lipped, teary and
rigid with fear. But despite her visible
pain and embarrassment she was determined to
rid herself of the memory of an event that
happened long ago and was the source of her
most disturbing nightmares and flashbacks.

Therapy session: Gag

S (extremely long pause) He put stuff in
my mouth and when I started to get sick he
held my mouth.

C He ejaculated in your mouth and made you
swallow it? Don't send your little girl
into that dark hole with that one!

S (choking and unable to talk)

C Did you feel like you were choking?

S (choking) I felt like I was throwing up.

C And then what happened?

S (choking) He wouldn't let me throw up
and I ended up swallowing it...(long silence)
.... then when he let me go I went into

the bathroom and I started throwing up and it
got all over me and I couldn't get it off. I
kept trying to get it all off and I couldn't
get it all off and I thought I had it all
off. I went to my room and there was more
and I went back to the bathroom and I tried
to get it off again and I kept going and
noticing more and more and more and I started
feeling frightened inside and crying because
I couldn't get it all off. It was all over
me and it was bad and I was ugly and dirty.
I didn't want it on me because it felt like
there was always more and more and more
and......(making hand gestures)......

    C Was it on your hands?

    S Yeah.......(crying).

    C It still feels like it's on there,
doesn't it? And you didn't think you'd ever
get it off.

    S When I tried to get it off it would get
all over my hands.

    C And you did that all by yourself didn't
you? No one to turn to and help you.
........(long silence).........Is there more?
Tell me the rest. You are doing very well,
being very brave. It takes a lot of courage
to say those things...to remember. They're
very horrible...very important.

    S (choking) I couldn't get it off and he
wasn't done...hoping he wouldn't see me......
made me go back in there. He wouldn't let
me wash it off. He said there was nothing to
wash off.

    C He wouldn't let you wash it off, so you
had to go to bed with it. Get in control of
your breathing...you know how. You don't
have to choke back anymore...................
........good....... you're doing very well.

S (choking) Feels like when I was choking
...he kept getting angry when I would start
to throw up.

C So then you had to deal with not only
him ejaculating in your mouth and feeling
sick but you had to deal with his anger
too..........(long silence).......this is
painful to look at. I can see why you have
been pushing your little girl in a hole,
because she kept trying to get you to look at
this one.

S She keeps trying to get it off of her
because it makes her feel gross and dirty,
and when I look at her I see all of the gross
stuff she couldn't wash off and I also see
all the different things she still feels.
Like she can't make him go away until it's
all gone............(getting lost in a
flashback)........

C Look around you...he's not here...look
at me...see...we're here...he's no longer a
threat to you. What he did was gross...the
feeling was disgusting, degrading. We're
here now...you've grown up and survived it
and you washed it off...you're here.

S (choking and crying) He kept holding my
mouth........ .....holding my
mouth...felt like he was trying to partly
keep my mouth shut and not let anything come
out and partly not let me breathe.....

C Do you feel like he was trying to kill
you?

S It felt like that...because he was angry
that I was throwing up.......I think he wanted to but stopped short of it always........
I kept wanting him to go ahead and do it so..
....

C So it would be over?

S   Yeah.......It still feels real "right
now"......the fear of him...the thing about
it is that it just seems that anything else I
could numb-out from...cope, kind of...and
THAT I couldn't move out and away...I could
not ....and besides feeling sick and frightened I felt overwhelmed.

C   Out of control...totally at his mercy.

S   Even when I was not in control, being
able to numb out was a little control, but
THEN I couldn't even do that.

C   And that was really scary being out of
control when your life was at stake.

S   (crying) That was so gross and bad that
that was one time that I really wanted to
die. The other times I was more afraid and I
didn't want him to hurt me or make me die.
But this time I wanted him to make me die...
because I felt like I could keep trying to
wash off the outside but the inside I could-
n't wash and it was all inside me. Sometimes
I still feel like...it just feels like
there's no way to get the grossness out of
me..................I'm feeling embarrassed!
......(long silence)........................
I was already feeling frightened because I
was trying to wash it off and I felt like I
got everything off...then he made me come out
and he did that to me and then it was overwhelming because now I know I'll never be
able to wash it all off.

C   It is horrible for a little girl to go
through that...degrading. And I feel no less
about you.

S   (avoiding eye contact) It just feels
like letting you see the grossness and the
nasty and the degrading stuff....you won't
want to look at me like I don't want to look
at me.

C No. You are not dirty. HE is gross and
disgusting and horrible.

S Sitting here, when you touch me I want
to move away, because I feel dirty, and say
"don't touch me!"

C I know. And I don't mind touching you.
You are not gross...HE is. HE did those
things. You were a pretty, innocent little
girl. HE did gross things to you. But it
didn't remain with you.

S It still feels like it.

C I'm sure it does. But you survived it
and now it's over.

S Inside and out I just feel coated with
all the...not only what he put on me but all
of the things he did to me. They are attached still. I feel like I walk around with
them.

C (taking Sheila's hands) Your hands are
not dirty. They look clean to me. There's
nothing there. I don't mind touching them.
You're very clean...there's nothing gross
there. You're o.k. You really are! You're
o.k.!

_____   _____

This therapy session clearly displays what I was feeling at the time - total disgust, humiliation and hurt. It's been a year since this particular session took place, yet as I try to read the transcript I am plagued with feelings of dirtiness, humiliation and hurt. However, as I write I am aware of a feeling that I didn't feel before - anger! Sometimes when I look at myself now I feel so inadequate. I feel as though I deserve bad things to happen to me. But when I remind myself that the actions of my stepfather were against a small child, not an adult, the anger, which all my life has been suppressed, begins to surface.

From a very early age I had tried so hard to be lovable and acceptable, but I couldn't seem to rate as much love as the pets in my home. I'm quite sure my parents have a different story. There have always been two stories; mine and theirs. Only mine, according to them, is a result of me living in a fantasy world. One not to be believed.

My parents would tell you that they always loved me and kept me safe, fed, and clothed. And it is true. I always had enough food to eat, clothes to wear, and a place to sleep. But the child in me still hurts from the absence of love and safety. Back then I needed so badly to feel love and safety that I looked for them in everything. I had even convinced myself that the restrictions set by my parents, to hide and protect the secret of my abuse, were really love, caring and safety. I think they too believed they were protecting me. And to some extent maybe they were. But what greater harm, short of death itself, could I have experienced more than that which I received in my own home.

Since my mom never told me that she hated me my feelings of not being loved had to be wrong. After all, all mothers love their children. And even though I can't remember my mom ever holding me, hugging me, or even touching me (except when I was bad)

she had to love me. After all, she didn't
give me away. Most of my life she seemed mad
at me, or at least irritated with me. But
that was only because I was so irritating to
be around. Otherwise she wouldn't have
treated me that way. After all, she didn't
treat my sisters or brother the way she
treated me. So I knew it wasn't her. It had
to be me. I had gotten only what I deserved.
My mom loved me!

And the safe feeling I needed, well....
my mom made sure that I came straight home
from school and played in a fenced yard until
I was thirteen. She never allowed me to spend
the night away from home or have friends
over. That's all because she was trying to
keep me safe from anyone or anything that
might hurt me.

On and on my childish rationale went.
"If it hurts, create an illusion." I made
the pain bearable. I covered and denied my
incest, my abuse and my emotional pain so I
could survive. And I did!

High Price to Pay

They said I was bad. They said I was re-
bellious.
When I cried out to be loved, they said I
was jealous.
The dishes aren't clean, your room is a
mess.
Compared to your sisters, you really are
less.

Why can't you be as good and kind?
Why is it you never mind?
You always get into trouble, you can't do
anything right.
Each thing we ask you to do, you always
put up a fight.

You didn't take care of your sister, and
now you drop your head.
And you should, for you know that it's your
fault she's dead.
You say you feel much hurt and pain?
Well all you should really feel is shame.
For after all, you are to blame.

Come now, let me teach you the facts of
life.
Come now, let me show you how to be a wife.
But I was only nine, I didn't want to know.
But he held tight, he wouldn't let me go.

The abuse went on both day and night.
Each waking hour filled with fright.
Now it's been eight years since I've moved
from home,
But in many ways the abuse goes on.

One deep feeling I'd like to express.
One more situation I'd like to address;
Though I may have been bad, still I must
say,
That the hell I now live in was a high
price to pay.

XI. HUGS, HOLDS AND SAFE TOUCHES

Therapy Session: The Chair

Children need to be hugged, caressed and cuddled. It is crucial to their survival. And little girls need this affection from their fathers as much as from their mothers. For father is the first male in a little girl's life. From him she will learn how to trust, share and develop relationships with all other men who will follow.

Incestuous fathers take advantage of this need. They see the longing in their little girls' eyes, sense their need for closeness, comfort and protection . . . and use it for their own personal, lustful gain.

Sheila's stepfather was no exception to this devastating misuse of power. In one of the most lengthy and difficult therapy sessions of all, Sheila opened up the deepest, gaping scar that remained with her from childhood. The scar that was created when her innocence and need were violated in the cruelest way.

--------------------   --------------------

Therapy session: The Chair

C   Let go of it with your words.

S   (lost in a flashback) He's got me . . . he keeps touching me and there's nobody else around . . .

C   Does he let go of you? . . . Do you want to stay with this and see if he does?....What happens?

S   (angry) I'm tired of staying stuck over there...I don't want to stay stuck over there anymore. . .

C   He's really got a hold on you.

151

S   He made me stay there a really long
time... my feet started to go numb.......
(long pause)...I can't go forward and
I can't go backwards...I'm stuck there.

C   Why are you staying there?

S   I can't move back.

C   Can you move forward? What happens?

S   I can't move forward 'cause I'll go
closer to him...can't move backwards 'cause
he won't let go.

C   You're stuck...you're totally at his
mercy...there isn't anything you can
do...you have to wait until he's
finished...

S   He won't let go.

C   Not a thing you can do...

S   If I pull away, he'll just squeeze . .

C   Tell me more.

S   He pulls me up in his lap, but it
doesn't feel safe like he wants to be good to
me and he keeps touching me more...

C   And what do you do then?

S   I don't do anything...I just stay
there...

C   You're trapped.

S   (in a flashback) If I got away I don't
know where I'd go 'cause I don't hear
anybody.

C   How do you feel? Tell me about it.
What are you looking at?

S   (confused) I can't see what she sees.
Usually I can see what she saw and now I
can't see what she saw...

C   Good. What does she feel? What are
you feeling now? How does it feel being
stuck in his lap?

S   I don't want to feel...I don't want
to feel...

C   What do you feel? You've got to
feel...It's the only way to get it out...

S   (anxious) I see him touch me...I don't
want to feel it.

C   How do you feel? What does it feel
like to still be stuck in his lap and
he's still not finished with you?

S   His hands are real hard, real hard
hands, real big, real hard hands, real big.

C   How does that feel having those big
hands rubbing over your body and there's no
one there to rescue you and you can't get
away?

S   It feels gross, feels gross...

C   You're feeling gross. What else?

S   (embarrassed) He's rough, he hurts....
at first he touches me and it feels scary,
but he gets rough.......I feel stupid.

C   It's embarrassing, isn't it?

S   I dont want to say what...

C   Those feelings are so embarrassing and
degrading.

S   (avoiding eye contact) I don't want to
say to you what he does.

C   Can you tell me what it feels like to
have him do those things to you?

S   (crying) I hurt...I burn...I feel gross
and dirty. I feel sad and degraded.

C   Give words to your tears.   What are
your tears trying to tell you?

S   (angry and crying) I want him to stop.

C   Go on...you're doing wonderfully.

S   (beats fists on thighs)

C   You're angry. You're mad at him
aren't you?

S   (choking) I'm mad at what he's doing to
her.

C   Don't choke it back.

S   He's hurting her and he doesn't know or
care...no one cares.

C   He's hurting YOU and doesn't care.
He doesn't even care.

S   (crying) She's little, he's big.

C   Yeah, it isn't fair.

S   It hurts really bad...(long pause)

C   Words?

S   (confused) I feel...she feels...I don't
want to say...I don't want to say...

C   You don't have to tell me.

S   I want to tell you. I don't want to feel the embarrassment.

C   What can we do to help you not feel embarrassed?

S   (long pause) Hold me and don't look at me.

C   (holding Sheila) You are not gross and you are not dirty. He is. Don't choke. You can talk now.

S   It sounds and feels real gross. It sounds and feels real, real gross.

C   I'm sure it does.

S   It's real gross.

C   He's a gross man.

S   No, REALLY gross.

C   He did really gross things to you.

S   When he...when he...when he touched me and hurt me...I feel like I...I feel hurt and burn and wet and I feel him touch me.......
(alot of choking)...he started touching me and I could feel the wet all over me again, but that time it was gross wet stuff all over me, but...(choking)...

C   Get in control. I'm with you. It's not happening now. You are in my office.

S   The wet was from ME not from him.

C   That scared you didn't it?

S   (crying) I just felt so gross. It just felt so gross and I was the gross one, not him! It was not from HIM on me, it was from ME on me. It felt all gross. It felt gross

like that time. It hurt. I hurt and burned
and the feeling...I didn't want to feel it.
I feel gross (choking).....He kept touching
me with his wet hands (choking)..........

   C   Get in control. You're in my office.
It's safe. He really degraded you.

   S   (choking and crying) I felt so gross.
Don't look at me. He said that the wetness
was from me, and I didn't want it to be from
me but I couldn't stop it. I couldn't make it
not be from me. I couldn't make him not
touch me. And then I felt like I couldn't be
away from the wet. I couldn't block. I
couldn't not feel it. When he let me go, I
had it all over me again...like before.

   C   I've got you...feel my arms. You're
not gross.

   S   (crying) There was wet sticky gross
stuff all over me.

   C   It was part of your normal body and he
turned it into something gross and degrading.
There's nothing gross about your body. It's
very normal.

   S   I felt ashamed and embarrassed because
I couldn't make it not be there. I felt real
dirty.

   C   There's nothing gross about you,
Sheila. He just made it seem that way. He
just made it seem that way. There's nothing
gross about you.

   S   Then, I wanted to cry and I couldn't
cry. Now, I'm crying inside and I can't cry.
I feel afraid and sad and embarrassed and
ashamed and I want...(long pause)........
I wanted to be held so bad, I kept almost
crying out for him to hold me and then
realizing I shouldn't do that, but I

wanted to be held. I was afraid and I wanted
to be held and I almost kept forgetting not
to let him hold me...that he was hurting me
(loud sigh).........

   C   And he knew that and took advantage.

   S   I felt real confused because I wanted
to move closer for him to hold me, and if I
tried to block out him touching me and
hurting me, then I wanted to move closer
and be held, and when I started to move
closer to be held, I was afraid because
he was touching me and hurting me.

   C   He really had you caught didn't he?
The only way you could get hugs was with
pain.

   S   (crying) I wanted the hugs real bad...
....I wanted them real bad........

   C   And you needed them and deserved them.

   S   I wanted him to hold me like he held my
sister, not like he held me. I wanted him to
hold me like he held her. He didn't hurt
her. She was happy and she trusted.

   C   I'd be angry. You wanted the same.

   S   I couldn't understand why he had to
hold me like that. He didn't hold her
like that. I don't understand why he
wouldn't hold me like he held her.

   C   I don't understand either because you
deserved it, too.

   S   (crying) I didn't try to be bad. I
didn't try to be different. I tried to be
just like her. I tried to be just like her
and do what she did...but he didn't act
like that to me.

C   And it's not because you didn't try.
God knows you tried.

S   (crying) I kept thinking that if I did
the exact things she did and acted just like
her then he'd hold me like he held her.

C   But that didn't work.

S   I'm tired. I don't want to be over
there with them anymore.

C   Then visualize him letting go of you...
getting off his lap....walking away....
You didn't ask for so much...just to be held.

S   He was the only one that held. Mom
never held. But when he held he touched. I
just wanted to be held. I just can't understand.

C   You'll never find a reason.

S   I just thought it was because I was
dirty and gross.

C   You're not gross and you never were and
it's not you. You've got to let go of that.
It's because of him. It's because of his
problems. It has nothing to do with you and
you need to let go of that and stop searching
for the logic in it.

S   I just feel mad if I didn't do anything
to make him do that.

C   That's right!!! That's exactly how it
should be!!!! There is no sense and no logic
and no matter how long you search, you are
not going to find it. He did it to you and
it doesn't make sense, and you have a right
to feel angry about that!!

———————   ———————

I was afraid to tell Charlotte that I really wanted my stepfather to hold me. I was afraid she would think I was strange to want to be close to someone who hurt me. Physical pain is scary, but emotional pain is incredibly worse. For while I had learned to numb my body, I couldn't numb my heart. I wanted so badly to be to my parents what my sister was...perfect, cute and cuddly.

I wish I could have felt what it was like to be that close to someone without feeling afraid or hurting. As I relived this flashback, like all the others, I was wishing I could forget it. But I couldn't. And even as I'm writing now, I see me as a small child, so confused and hurting that I would have burst into tears if it weren't for being too afraid. Then I see him reach his hand towards me. I feel his touch. I close my eyes and try to numb-out. But I don't, because I want to feel him hold me, not hurt me, hold me. I am distracted by the desire to be held, which forces me to feel the pain of his abuse.

It is hard to write this and it feels so real that I am left with only one thought. It is the same thought I had back then. "Please hold me how it doesn't hurt."

Touch, in the form of hugs, holds and safe touches became a vital part of therapy for Sheila. In the beginning when I would touch her arm during a session, her eyes would immediately flash up to mine with a confused look of fear, suspicion and relief. She seemed to be working hard on discriminating whether my touch was part of a flashback or if it was really me, the therapist she wanted so badly to trust.

I tried to remember to touch Sheila in small ways as often as possible. Usually that meant gently putting my hand on her shoulder, hand or knee. I persisted in

touching despite her visible ambivalence and
she soon came to not only enjoy my touch, but
to hunger for it. She found strength and
security from the simple warmth of another
human being.

Touch has now become a vital part of
Sheila's life. Our therapy sessions always
end with a ritual hug, and Sheila doesn't
hesitate to remind me if I forget. One day
she hesitantly asked me if I would place one
of my hands on the side or back of her head
when I hugged her. She said this helped her
feel the hug more quickly. I was so proud of
her courage in asking directly for what she
needed; something extremely difficult for
most incest survivors. And Sheila has learned
not only how to find comforting touch for
herself and to hold herself when no one else
is around, but she is now able to reach out
to her children and give them the kind of
touch she never experienced as a child.
Solid, positive change has clearly taken
place in her life.

———————   ———————

This Kind of Touch

Tonight as I lay awake in bed,
  my hands propped beneath my head,
Afraid to close my eyes to sleep,
    for fear that into my room he'll creep.
I see him standing at my door,
    as he has so many nights before.
He doesn't think I know he's there;
    he doesn't know I see him stare.
And as he moves beside my bed,
    his ugly touch I start to dread.
For I feel frightened when I see his hand
    reaching out, touching me.
And I think that if I'd never been
    touched, it would have been better
Than this kind of touch.

Rules of the Corner

Sit quietly, child, and listen;
Dare not speak a word.
For danger may await you if by chance
  you're heard.

Sit tightly in a corner,
With your knees pulled to your chest;
This way you can hold you and maybe
    you can rest.

Never go to this corner
If you're being eyed;
For this safe corner becomes a trap
If here, by him, you're spied.

Bring with you to this corner
All your tears and pain,
For this is a place you can be held
As long as you remain.

The tighter that you hold you
The safer you can feel,
And hopefully before you leave
Some inside wound can heal.

This corner has no magic power,
And is never safe past half an hour;
Yet sheltered by it you can be,
Just lean back and you will see.

———————   ———————

XII. I AM AN
INCEST VICTIM???

Therapy Session: Carol's call

Sheila spent month after month purging herself of terrors from the past. And while she felt a little more cleansed each time, the work remained extremely difficult. I admired the courage it must have taken her each week to walk into my office, sit down on that same wicker chair with all its old associations, and begin one more time to give painful, graphic accounts of her tortuous past.

Life in general seemed to be going better for Sheila. She had regained control of her parenting role, as was clearly reflected in the dramatic change in her children's behavior. The girls smiled easily and were more spontaneous. But most importantly, they were no longer afraid to express their anger - loud and clear!

The other improvements in Sheila's life centered around the increase in her self-esteem and self-confidence. She had lost thirty-six pounds, was wearing make-up and colorful clothes, and had developed close friendships with some very supportive and caring women in her life.

Sheila had struggled hard to reach this point in her growth and she seemed to be enjoying, with some suspicion, this new experience of life. For me it was fulfilling to see her so happy. But I wasn't sure how long this pleasant plateau would last. The consistent purging had lessened the stress in Sheila's daily life and helped her carry on in a more normal fashion. But her work was not finished. For each time she revealed another episode of incest from her past, she would also carefully sift through the ruins, grabbing at any evidence she could find that would magically wisk her away from the frightening truth - that it wasn't her fault. The truth that would inevitably bring forth

screaming rage and anger - anger that would
not be directed toward herself but at her
stepfather, her mother and the whole atrocity
that she, as an innocent little girl, was
once forced to endure.

———————   ———————

The Child in Me

I didn't stop it because I didn't talk,

or maybe it's the way I walk.

Whose fault was it? Yours or mine?

I drudge through my past to find a

sign.

Each time I say it was his fault,

some inside voice speaks out.

One small forgotten issue

that seems to raise some doubt.

Who is that voice inside of me

that refuses to let my innocence be?

I thought it was those criticizing words,

that as a child I always heard.

But surprised I was to come to see

they're words of the little child in

me.

———————   ———————

What happened next in the fascinating
journey down Sheila's road to recovery will
always remind me to maintain a humble perspective on my ability to change human behavior. I had slowly and gently been trying
for weeks to help Sheila explore the conse-
quences of inevitably accepting the truth of
her past - to help her see her choices more
clearly and how they would affect her life.
But she was too frightened to even look.
Then, BAM! Out of nowhere came a phone call
to Sheila from a sister I didn't know even
existed. The impact of that call led Sheila,
or rather forced Sheila, further down her
road to recovery than anything I'd said in
months. The timing of the call was so
incredible and it shifted Sheila's gears with
such force and speed that it left her reeling
and spinning for weeks.

————————   ————————

Therapy session: Carol's Call

S   Carol said, "I wanna ask you something point blank. Did Joe ever rape you?"
I just burst into tears and I said "I don't want to hear about it! I don't want to say anything about it, I don't want to say anything about it, I don't want to talk about it, just drop it!" Then I said "Yes" and she started crying and said "He did me too!"

C   Sheila!

S   She said that she was sorry that she left me behind.   She didn't think it would happen to anybody else. She said that was why she ran away.   She said her counselors didn't believe her. She told her husband and he told her she caused it because she was a tramp. (Crying) I'm feeling such mixed feelings because I'm mixed between being mad at her for leaving me and not wanting to believe her. I don't want to believe her because it makes it too valid.

C   It did happen to two people in the family. He is a child molester.

S   I just don't want to believe her.

C   Why do you insist on not believing it? What do you gain?

S   It just felt like, when she said that, all of it came flooding in.

C   She made it real. It wasn't just you.

S   I feel angry and guilty at the same time. I don't want to believe her.

C   I understand that.

S   It just kind of takes apart the whole thing for me. I feel like...like all my feeling of control, survival...everything was rooted in it just being me. It's only me, it's only something about me...see it didn't happen to anyone else!

C   It was me, and therefore, if I change, it won't be me?

S   Now it feels like, like I should feel better but I don't.

C   And maybe some day you will. Right now you don't.

S   I was angry at her for asking me that! I didn't want her to ask me that!

C   You want to keep that illusion - the illusion that has kept you comfortable - not happy. But it is an illusion, Sheila. One that you created back when you reached out to your mother and realized she wasn't there. You've lived with that illusion for about twenty-five years now, and Carol broke right through it.

S   I just feel like, "How dare you break that for me, you're not even here, you're way out there, you don't even know me, and you come into my life and just.....(crying). It feels like she has undone the only way I knew how to deal with it. I hurt so badly inside and felt degraded. I just wanted it to end so no one else would have control over me! I don't want to find out any more! Just when I think I'm done, something else! (crying)

C   So tell me why you didn't end the conversation.

S   I was afraid to. I didn't want to hurt her. She was trying to be really nice to me,

supportive. I ended the conversation
quickly, though. I'm having a hard time
not blaming her. It wasn't her, it was
my stepfather, but I have a hard time not
blaming her because I feel like it started
with her.

   C   You just have a real hard time being
angry at him, don't you? You are real
invested in bailing him out. He never
gets any blame put on him at all. It's
Carol's fault, it's your fault, but it's
never Joe's fault. Once you came close to
talking about how you'd like to dig your
fingernails into him, but you bounced right
off of it. You won't stay on it for a
second. Be aware of that.

   S   I think somehow I have him innocent
until I totally prove him guilty, and me
guilty until I totally prove me innocent.

   C   Why do you give him such a break?

   S   Because I felt so guilty. How could I
be guilty and he be guilty, too? I think
that for so long he convinced me it had
nothing to do with him that it's hard to
take that out and change it all around. If I
didn't believe in my head I should be angry,
I would say those feelings don't exist. I
feel like Carol and I are the only ones that
are black sheep and I keep feeling like it's
because of what we did.

   C   You can get caught up in that, and
that's a choice you make. You can choose to
get caught up into thinking, "that's why we
got molested, because we were the black
sheep" or you can think "we're the ones
that can't stand being in the family because
of what happened to us." You'll never be
able to prove it. You can search your memory
banks until you're blue in the face. You can
talk to everyone else. But you're not going

to be able to prove it. You can make a
choice what to believe or not. Or, make a
choice to stay hung up on it, never know,
and never get yourself off the hook and
be unhappy always wondering, "What did I do?"
And that comes back to your issue of control.
You had no control over what happened then.
It happened, you had no control and you
created an illusion that you did. You have a
hard choice to make; the choice Carol threw
in your face last night. You can choose to
hold on to your illusion of control or just
accept the fact you never had control.
There's nothing you could have done to make
it different, there's nothing you can do now
to make it different. It happened and it's
part of you.

S   It feels like I've had choices before,
but this time the choice isn't really there.

C   Why?

S   Because I don't think I could stay with
the illusion.

C   Today you are an incest survivor?

S   Even when I went to the AMAC group I
would sit in there, but I felt like they were
all...and I wasn't........

C   The jury was still out on you. How
did you feel about them?

S   Sometimes I had to fight wondering what
they did or didn't do.

C   I've known for two years that you are
an incest survivor. I was still interested,
and remain so two years later, in being
involved with you. No one has the trouble
with you that you have.

S   I can't stop feeling gross.

C   This is a new day. Today you're an incest survivor. The jury is in. Carol
basically pronounced the verdict.

S   No one elected her jury!

C   But she spoke for the jury and read the
verdict. It said "Sheila Sisk is an incest
survivor."

S   It felt more like "Sheila Sisk,guilty!"

C   That's what you do with it. Maybe you
just need to feel gross for a while longer.
That doesn't mean the rest of the world
thinks you're gross.

S   I'm feeling real bogged down.

C   You got a heap of reality dumped on
you. I'll bet you're feeling bogged down.
That's an awful lot to deal with. I want
you to do two things this week. First, be
o.k. with being angry at Carol and realize
that when you're feeling angry, that's when
you're healthy. Not necessarily happy. But
this isn't an ideal world where you can be
happy all the time. Second, start saying to
yourself out loud, "I'm an incest survivor."
Say it to me now. I won't walk out on you.

S   (pause) "I'm an incest survivor." I
don't want to say it! It feels like I'm
saying, "I'm gross."

C   HE is gross! "I'm an incest survivor
and gross things were done to me." Say it
that way, desensitize yourself.

S   (rapidly and looking at the floor) "I'm
an incest survivor and gross things were done
to me."

C   Tell me. Look at me and tell me.

174

S   I'm an......

C   Look at me.

S   I don't want you to see me that way.

C   I want you to look at me and say it.

S   I don't want you to look at me like an incest survivor...like I have a disease.

C   I want you to see how I look at you when you say it, because I'm not looking at you that way. You're looking at you that way. I want you to see that nothing changes when you tell me.

S   (looking at Charlotte) "I'm an incest survivor."

C   I know, and I love you anyway, and I love you FOR that - for all the courage it took you to go through that. (Hug...)

I never realized how hard it could be to say "I am an incest survivor," yet every time I tried to say it I struggled with the words. Finally I managed to say it. "I am....an.... incest survivor." But I felt as though I had just written the sentence across my chest. So I quickly removed it from my thoughts as soon as the session ended. It was just too scary and felt too degrading. Somehow I felt that by not owning the statement I could not own the incest. It had taken me a long time before I could even say I was an incest sur- vivor, but I knew in my gut I really wasn't accepting it. I was trying, but all it seemed to mean was more pain, more despair, and more hard work.

Talking about my incest was hard, but believing it seemed impossible. Saying the sentence was a good start, though, for now my head had heard me say it and I knew I could never forget the sound of it. And now I had something I could take with the ugliness I felt the first time I said "I am an incest survivor." For Charlotte's words that quickly followed seemed to melt some of the pain and ugliness, and I could never forget those words: "I know and I love you anyway!"

_____   _____

XIII. THE DYING ILLUSION

Therapy Session: Reality

Phone calls with Carol continued to take place and move Sheila at an accelerated rate toward facing the inevitable. I watched as she approached her fate with great ambivalence. She felt relief at the possibility of finally settling into a place in her life based on reality and honesty; a place where she would no longer need to deny her past and spin complicated webs trying to deceive herself. But she also felt fear and terror as she approached a place in her life where there would no longer be barriers to the long-held, festering anger she felt toward her parents.

Sheila became painfully aware of her ambivalence after another call with Carol catapulted her even further into her future.

Therapy session: Reality

S   She said he would walk in on her a lot when she was dressing in the bathroom and he'd say "Oops, excuse me babygal. I didn't know you were in here." The one thing that's really hard is that . . . .I feel like my emotions and words are stuck in the same place and I can't get one out without the other. I'm just tired of crying because of him!

C   Yeah! Now that's an honest statement!

S   He used to call us all babygal. I knew when he called me that he was trying to coax me and entice me and get me to come near him to be comforted or held. That was like a key word. I hadn't even heard him say that in so long. I'd even forgotten that word.

It's not even a word, it's his own little pet thing. I'd forgotten until she said that. Up until then when she was talking I figured all of this story anyone could figure out. And then she said "babygal!"

C   It happened and he did it.

S   Carol said she got in trouble for not getting home 'til 10 p.m. Then later when she didn't want him to touch her he'd ask her if she wanted him to tell my mom what she and her date had been doing, and that he knew what they had been up to. And if my mom took her to the doctor, then they definitely would know what she had been up to, saying that her date had done what HE'd really done to her!

C   Now do you see how diabolical his mind is and how he sets people up? That was such a set up! And there was nothing she could do about it. Do you see how warped his mind is? Do you think that at three years of age you could have found any way around him? He did the same thing to you. He set you up and had it well planned in advance. There is no way a small child could manipulate around that. You were just a little girl!

S   When I started questioning what he was doing, he said he had to teach me what men do. We had been out in the yard playing and some Navy guys were out there and he said he had to teach me what they could do.

C   Yeah, I've heard that one a hundred times. That is a classical line from a sex offender, and little girls are no match for that.

S   I wanted to find some fault with Carol's story because I wanted to find a rea-son why she could have stopped it. She was a lot older and if she couldn't have stopped it then....it kind of blows another illusion. I feel jumpy and stupid. I'm stuck.

C   How long are you going to stay stuck
there?

S   I think I'm so afraid that confronting
my family is inevitable that I want to do
what I can to find any possible doubt, because I know they're going to deny it again.

C   Yes, they are.

S   And I don't want any doubt in me to
latch onto their denial and push me back into
it.

C   Yeah, I hear that.

S   (crying) Because I believed me when I
went to my mom and told her, but when I left
her after trying to tell her, I started not
believing me.

C   That was a real turning point for you
in your life.

S   (crying) It was when I decided that it
didn't happen, or that I had to believe it
didn't happen. Plus, my mom was always so
right in what she said that I had to be
wrong. If she said it didn't happen, then
it didn't happen!

C   You've come so far in undoing that,
and you don't want to go back to that point
again.

S   On the outside, I'm really tough to my
family and I tell them "I don't kiss ass anymore," but on the inside I'm still so afraid.
I'm not afraid of what they can do to me on
the outside, but emotionally.

C   What she did to you that one day, by
denying it, you've been fighting for years to

undo, putting it to every test possible to convince yourself she's wrong and you're right.

S   At the time, my mom could do no wrong. She was perfect. She knew everything. She had all the right answers. I know there's a strong possibility of it all coming out and it's made me real aware that I fear them a lot. Not like in the beginning, but still I have a real big fear. I used to think it was because they'd all turn their back on me and I wouldn't have them anymore. But I think it's the denial itself. I don't think it's the fear of losing them, because I don't really have them. I think it's the fear of losing me....

C   And you've struggled so hard to find yourself.

S   I remember feeling back then it was in-evitable that it was going to come out. It was happening too much and he wasn't hiding it good enough. I don't know if I was just feeling like I wanted to tell that bad or what. But finally it came out, and then the BIG DENIAL....and now it feels like the same thing prefacing up to another big denial.

C   I can tell you that when and if it comes out again, they will deny it. I can guarantee you they will deny it. But that doesn't mean it didn't happen. It just means they are choosing to deny it.

S   They'll say Carol and I collaborated.

C   Even if you hadn't talked with her, they'd find another reason to deny it. Why would they own up to it? Do you think Joe's going to own up to all that? Molesting two of his daughters? No way! Do you think your mom's gonna own up to not protecting you? No way! They will deny it, and that doesn't

mean it didn't happen. That is just how they
choose to deal with it.

   S   That day she denied it...and I denied
it too....there was part of me inside that
just screamed. I think that's when the child
in me retreated way back down.

   C   Feelings didn't have anything to do
with reality or survival, did they? You had
to take on your mom's feelings and percep-
tions.

   S   My child wanted somebody to be there
for her. My adult said it really was my
fault, and then my child coaxed her to tell.
And then the denial, and my child just went
right down....and my child was screaming.....

C   I think your little-girl-feelings are
the same as they were then - just screaming
out for someone to be there. And I think
that's why you've been letting your little-
girl-feelings surface. You've found a safe
place to scream out.

S   Why can't I just let it drop, let it
die? They're just going to deny it. If I
drop it now, maybe it won't come out.

C   Why won't you drop it?

S   Because I think if I drop it, a part of
me is dropped.

C   That's right, and you're sick and tired
of living as half a person, particularly
when it's been done in the name of incest!

S   (crying) I know now why I have to say I
am an incest survivor; because a part of me
is attached to that and if I can't say that,
then I can't have that part of me.

C   Yeah, that is very real.

S   For a long time, I've been willing to
give up that part of me, but the incest
attached itself to a very vital part of me...
(long pause). This whole week I've felt like
someone died. I've been down and real des-
pondent and real teary - like when my sister
died, I felt breath-taking down.

C   I wonder who died, or what?

S   A part of me. I wish it were the child.

C   Which part was it?

S   The part that held the illusion. The
part that's tough, strong and kept the child
manipulated and the adult alive. The part I
felt like I needed worse than me as a child.

Not You But I

You're the one who made me hurt,
  Yet I'm the one who feels like dirt.
You're the one who is to blame,
  Yet I'm the one who lives in shame.
You're the cause of my nightmares,
  Yet I lay awake trembling, but what
    do you care?
And when I'd told what you had done,
  I'm the one mom chose to shun.
You're the one who made me cry,
  Then dared a tear to leave my eye.
How tough, how strong you must have been,
  You had total control when I was ten.

I began to try to sort through all my
feelings. Had my mom really denied the abuse
or maybe she really didn't see what was happening to me. I began to hear myself trying
to rationalize everything out in my head. I
wanted badly to know the answers but I wasn't
about to ask. I decided to write what I
would some day like my mom to know but was
too afraid to tell her now.

Mom,

    I'm writing this to you though I know
I'll never give it to you directly because I'm still too afraid. I know this
will hurt you, but I hurt too. I'm sure
you'll understand though, for it's like
you used to tell me when you hit me. You
would cry and tell me how it hurt you
more than it did me. Well physically you
were right, because there came a time
when you couldn't hurt my body any more.
I learned to have power over the pain.
I felt the first hit and I said to myself, this doesn't hurt, and then I would
stand until you finished hitting me.
    I watched the anger in your eyes that
scared me, and I hurt inside. But Mom,
the thing that hurt the most was the
beatings and criticism I received because
he thought I was so bad. He said to me
often, "If it wasn't for you, your mother
and I would never fight." I would have
left, but I didn't know where to go, and
I was afraid he might hurt you when he
was drinking. I remember when I would
just walk through the room, he would look
at me with hate and sigh loud with disgust. I used to want so badly for him to
like me like he did my sister. He was
always telling me how childish I was acting and that I wasn't acting any more
grown up than the younger ones. But,
Mom, I was a child.
    Then when Ann was born with hydro-

cephalus and Joe came home and told us that something was wrong, I went to my room and buried my face in my pillow and cried. All I could think about was the many nights I sat awake listening to the two of you fight. He would hit and shove and you would shove back. For two-and-a-half years I helped the best I could to take care of the baby. I was only ten when she was born, but I fed, changed and gave her her medicines. When you were in the hospital, I took care of her with very little help. Mom, I was so scared I'd do something wrong, or she might die. I was afraid I wouldn't know what to do. And I got tired too - so tired of holding her and taking care of her. I loved her, but I wanted so badly to play. Then when she died, I hurt so badly because I felt like the only person who had ever loved or needed me had just died. I ran out and beat a tree with my fist trying not to cry, trying to pretend it was a dream.

Later Joe told me that it was my fault she died, because I dragged her all over the yard and because I always made you fuss and fight with me, upsetting Ann. I wasn't meaning to drag her around the yard. I just wanted to show her off to the neighbors. I really believed I made her die. I hated me for that.

Mom, do you remember when I came to you and told you that Joe had been bothering me, touching me, using me? I explained the best I knew how. I didn't know what words to use to tell you what he was doing to me. At first you acted very concerned and you questioned me intently with questions like "What did he have on?" and "Are you sure?" and "What did you do?" Mom, I was so scared and embarrassed to begin with, but as you tried to pin me down to details of what seemed like a whole lifetime of experiences, and he came in the room, I got

even more scared. I saw him looking at
me and then I heard him deny it to you.
I knew you would believe him over me.
You always had. So, I denied it, too. It
just wasn't worth the embarrassment and
pain of trying to convince you, nor was
it worth the fear I felt when I looked
into his eyes. Then you asked me what I
wanted you to do, get a divorce? Mom, I
didn't want you to do anything except believe me and make him leave me alone.
Then I heard you call others in the family. Each time the call would begin,
"Guess what Sheila said?" Mom, you did
not believe me then, and you probably
won't now, but I'm trying to begin to believe myself again.

That day when you didn't believe me,
part of me went screaming and crying so
deep inside myself that I thought I
would never find me again. Through the
years, your questions about what's going
on with me, or what ever could be so bad
to make me try to kill myself, and your
statements about how you've always been
so close to all of your children, have
continued to deny the sexual abuse I experienced from him.

Remember a year ago, the night you
came walking into my house to let me
know that you had my children and I
wasn't getting them back until I could
straighten up? You said I was acting
like a crazy person because I had lost my
temper and thrown a few things. And I
had cut myself, and that was insane, and
I needed help. I was too hurt and afraid
to tell you that I hated me so badly because I saw myself taking my anger out on
my children like you had me. I was
too afraid to tell you that I cut myself
trying to cut away and block out the
grossness and dirtiness I felt for what
he had done to me.

Mom, I could go on and on, but if you
can't hear me by now, like you couldn't
hear me then, you probably never will.
That hurts really badly. I'll close this
letter now, but I will never again close
my memory.

Sheila

What I Meant To Do

I meant to push him away you see,

   but he seemed so big and scary to me.

I meant to run and hide from him,

   but he'd only call me out again.

I meant to tell him to leave me alone,

   'cause what he was doing to me felt

   wrong.

I meant to tell what he had done,

   but I didn't 'cause I had no one.

XIV. I AM AN INCEST SURVIVOR!!!

"It was ME he hurt! It was ME!!!"

Several months after the writing of my "letter to mom" I came home from a very long day. It was one of those days where I tried to do too much, too well, too fast, when I was too tired. As I walked in the door, the phone was ringing. I answered it and it was my mom.

"Sheila, what are you doing this evening?" she asked.

"Ummmm, I'm not sure. What do you ..."

"Well let me just tell you what I need you to do."

She went on to tell me that she needed me to use the ladder I had borrowed from her to fix an overhead light plug in her home.

"I need you to fix it before he (stepfather) tries to stubbornly climb up and do it and ends up falling. If he falls I won't be able to get him up by myself."

I told her that I had just walked in the door but I would come as soon as I had the girls settled at home. I didn't want to go to my mom's, yet I felt like I should since I had their ladder. I was wishing so badly I had returned it earlier. The phone rang and interrupted my thoughts. It was mom again.

"Sheila! Do you know how much longer you are going to be? I'm afraid he's going to try to do it himself. He's ranting and raving and being so stubborn!"

"I'm leaving in fifteen minutes! It's not hurting anything or an emergency that I do it this instant, is it?" I questioned.

193

I hung up the phone and got ready to leave the house, but just as I was walking out the door the phone rang again.

"Sheila! (screaming and crying) You bring that damn ladder right now or I'll come get it myself if I have to walk and get it!! He has ranted and raved around here about how he can't do this and can't do that and I've caught hell because you're not here with that damn ladder. I've always caught hell for everyone and I'm tired of catching hell for you!"

"I'm on my way!"

She hung up and I slammed down the phone, grabbed the ladder, threw it in the car and sped over there. On the way I felt so angry. I cussed and called them names and tried to think how I could most angrily pitch the ladder into the yard and speed off. But when I drove up mom was standing in the yard. I panicked! I couldn't think! I didn't know what to say! I felt afraid and was trembling. I took the ladder and walked to the gate where she was standing. I hated me. There I stood again at her beckoning call; to serve him and her at my expense. Then my words betrayed me.

"Do you still want me to fix it for you?"

"No. Just put the ladder in the porch." she snapped. "I don't know what I should do with him. Sometimes I feel like divorcing him."

"You should." I said quietly.

I opened the door, but as I walked in, the anger and rage I had felt in the car suddenly returned. I decided to go into the room where Joe was sitting and slam the ladder down and say "There's your ladder!" and

stomp out. But when I put the ladder down I
set it the wrong way and had to turn quickly
to stop it from falling. Then I realized I
had my back to him and I was too close! I
felt trapped and scared! My whole being
screamed inside. I turned around, and for
the first time stood face to face, just inches away, from my molester!! Always before
when I would see him I would see a disgusting
and dirty man who I knew had molested a child
and I felt sick when I looked at him. This
time was different. He wasn't just a molester, he was MY molester! I am an incest survivor because he molested ME! I feel dirty,
ugly, shame, disgrace, humiliation, pain and
terror because HE hurt ME! HE hurt ME when I
was a child! It was ME he hurt! It was ME!!
It was me years ago that he had molested and
it was me NOW!

It was as if each painful memory had
ripped off a part of me and I had left those
parts behind. And now the memory had snapped
back to me with each part. And all of the
pain from then and now totally encompassed
me. The man who had for years molested my
body, my mind and my very being was just
inches away from me! I couldn't say anything! I just fled out of there like a bat
out of hell. I drove and drove and don't
even remember how I had gotten out of there.
All I could see for that instant was HIM.
Not him who molested a child but HIM who
molested ME! I cried and screamed in fear
and terror like I never had before. My body
trembled and shook like it did every time he
molested me. I couldn't seem to get far
enough away fast enough. He had molested me
when I was a small child. He had molested me
continuously through the years into my teens.
And now, in my gut, I felt as if he had just
done it again. And I couldn't protect the
little girl inside any more. I couldn't tell
her all those disgusting things had not happened. For she and I both knew the truth now.
She felt it. I felt it. We felt it together!

——————— ———————

That day at her parents' house Sheila had a brief flash of integration and it scared her beyond her wildest imagination. It had been so long since she had felt whole and in complete unity with herself. She almost did not recognize it. She felt what she would have felt as a child, in the room with her stepfather, had her defense mechanisms not had to separate out the pain so she could merely survive.

Now the hardest work of all could begin for Sheila. The work that she had been leading up to for years. For now she could not only continue recalling the events of the past, she could re-experience them as well. The pain that had been detached for all the years of her childhood would now be flooding in. The pain she had set aside, in order to merely survive, would be coming out. She would be feeling it like she never had before.

——————— ———————

All those fragmented pieces of me, ripped off by the horrible memories of my past and left behind, had suddenly returned. And they were so close I couldn't run from them anymore. The illusion of self-blame and denial I had created to hide behind, had been forced out by the startling reality of my face-to-face experience with my molester, and my fragmented pieces took their proper place.

Now there was a different, painful battle raging inside of me. I couldn't run from the pain of my memories anymore. I had to stay and feel them, for there was no longer an illusion to safely run to. And the memories were no longer pencil-sketched skeletons of my past, but were complete with color, sound and dimension. The fragmented pieces of me provided each painful memory

196

with searing emotions; anger, fear, sadness, embarrassment and hurt more painful than I had ever experienced before. And they were seething within me.

XV. THE LIGHT

"Wholeness, self-forgiveness and self-love."

The acceptance of my incest has by far been the hardest, most painful reality I have dealt with throughout my entire therapy. No more illusions or denial to protect me. No more self-blame to block the anger inside me. The anger and hurt had been there since I was a child and much still remains. But I have begun the healthiest part of my recovery. It is as if I have journeyed for three years to get to this place of finding me. And though it is painful and scary to see my unleashed anger and rage, and experience the bitter reality of my incest without self-blame or illusion, I believe I will survive this part of my recovery, for I survived incest.

The scope of Sheila's anger was truly overwhelming. The black and white sketches she had previously recalled of her past were now being filled in with flaming, screaming, angry color. That anger had been inside for years and was now surging forth with great force and velocity.

Sheila was afraid of this voyage into the darkness inside herself. She was afraid it would grab hold and destroy her; that she would become self-destructive again or go crazy, or that she would never again surface to see the light of day.

She despaired over the sight of yet another hurdle to climb to reach her goal of wholeness. She had climbed so many. Now another? "Why?" she asked. And she was right when she said it wasn't fair. After spending years of tormenting work, her reward for finally accepting the fact of her incest and her innocence was another hurdle! But not just "another" hurdle, the biggest hurdle of all.

"It isn't fair! Why must my hard work be rewarded with more pain and humiliation? Why must I return to his bed to be raped once more? Why must the horrible memories of my incest continue to drag me back to be violated and destroyed by him? Will I ever be free to live a life without pain?" I tearfully questioned Charlotte, begging for answers to my continued struggle.

"Sheila, you don't have to run anymore" she replied. "You are not a child and he has no control over you any more. You can feel this time; be angry, hate, hit, scream and cry until you have no more tears left to cry. You can be in control this time. Don't let him have the control any more. Be angry! Scream with rage! Cry!"

Charlotte was right. My stepfather is now seventy-nine years old. He is fatally ill and his days are numbered. He can't hurt me any more. I don't have to relive my past. But I will have to re-experience the pain of it through my memories as I rip them away with my anger and give power through words to my gathered fragments. I will soothe and heal my wounds with my tears and reunite my fragments through self-acceptance and self-love. And I know Charlotte will be at my side, ready to provide safe hugs, holds and touches, and encourage me to go on.

———————   ———————

I believed that the final acceptance and expression of her pain and rage would be her last remaining hurdle for her recovery from her incestuous past. I told her that I believed that. And I told her that I would be there with her through the darkness and be there when she reached the other side. She had gone through so much alone. She deserved to have the assurance of my hand to reach for when her fears of insanity threatened.

I'm not sure where Sheila ever found the courage to live out her life - from the time she was three years old and the abuse of her body and soul began, to her young adult years and having to cope with raising two small children alone, to her first step into therapy as she attempted to face the monster inside herself, right up to the past three years of hellish work in intense therapy. But wherever she originally found the courage, she secretly returned to that source and found more.

Sheila now speaks of anger so awesome and vivid it cannot be captured with words. Anger that screams, cries, sickens, destroys, suffocates and overwhelms. Anger that is felt in every part of the body, mind and spirit. Anger that feels as if it will last through eternity. Anger that must have expression and must not because it is dark, ugly and capable of unspeakable destruction.

I agonize as I listen to incomprehensible pain and anger. But I also silently shout for joy as I watch the pain slowly, one word, one tear, one tremble at a time being forced out, never again to haunt and destroy.

Sheila is in the most terrifying and crucial phase of her recovery and she struggles daily to continue. But with every step she takes into her darkness I can clearly see her coming closer and closer to her light. She can only vaguely see this, but each week as I watch her stare her dark and ugly monster of anger straight in the eyes, describe it, size it up, touch it, scream at it, cry in front of it, and refuse to run away from it, I see the light slowly but surely beginning to shine on her. And it is the light of wholeness, self-forgiveness and self-love.

I have felt incredibly fortunate to have taken this journey and to have learned along the way with Sheila. It has been wonderful to see the blossoming of a young woman who will someday be able to reach her potential and become the person she was fully meant to be. And I've seen something else wonderful happen that has given so much more meaning to this experience, and that is the blossoming of Sheila's two children. They will be here long after Sheila is gone. They are what she will leave behind - the fruits of her labor.

I was never so struck with this realization than on one cool Florida winter day. I was sitting in Sheila's home and the popular Whitney Houston hit, "The Greatest Love of All" came on the radio. It was Sheila's favorite song. She said it made her think of her own childhood; never believing she was loveable and wanting so badly for someone to be proud of her and love her for who she was. But mostly the song reminded her that she never wanted her girls to experience the painful striving and longing she had, for a love that was never to come.

The two girls chimed in singing just as naturally as if they had written the lyrics themselves. I knew then that change at the most important level - the future - had already taken place. I knew that Heather and Hannah would never have to experience the loss of innocence and joy that Sheila had as a child. And as their little care-free spirits sang and danced to that lovely, inspiring song, I felt so very happy. Little did they know how much that song meant to their mother as she journeyed on her rocky road to recovery, and that because of her tremendous courage, it need never mean the same to them.

——————— ———————

I wanted to change. I wanted to stop living in fear. I wanted the deep, agonizing pain and humiliation to go away. So I found someone who could and would believe in me, even when I couldn't believe in myself. Someone who cared enough about me to go with me through the hell inside.

Neither Charlotte or I could see what the next turn would hold. But somewhere deep inside we both knew there was a frightened child and a stifled adult trying to find a way out. I was stumbling and hurting through a hell that seemingly had no end. And Charlotte not only walked down the dimly lit hallways of my past, but held my hand as I walked along-side her. And when I tripped on brutal reality and painful memories, she slowed up until I could get to my feet. At times she had to bend and give more than one could ever demand of anyone, to help me on my way down the hallway that will lead to my resolution.

I will never forget the hell I endured as a child, but I will never live in it again. I cannot imagine a greater hell than that inner hell placed within the very being of a child by its parents.

I will never regret or forget the painful, hard work of therapy for it has purchased my recovery. Recovery that will someday be total. And I will never forget Charlotte, who is continually faced with reasons for giving up. But she chooses to look beyond my walls that push her away, sees me struggling, and extends her hand to me.

This is a therapist, my friend

A great respect I have for you
    for all the pain you've walked me
    through.

Your caring voice I've learned to hear
    has helped me face a lot of fear.

Your eyes reveal your understanding.
    You gently encourage without demanding.

In the past three years I've come to see
    just how much you believe in me.

Your consistency has built in me
a new sense of stability.

And I'll trust you more as you continue
to be totally up-front and honest with
me.

For my work is not done we're both aware,
but it's been three years
and you're still there.

    Both incest and recovery are equally
hard, but incest is alone. Recovery is not.
My recovery involved re-experiencing my pain.
But when it became too intense or the hallways too long and dark, this time there was a
hand to reach for, safe arms to hold me until
I stopped trembling, and a gentle, familiar
voice to encourage me, making the pain of
incest bearable and recovery possible.

XVI. THE DREAM

"There is a door!
There really is a door!"

Charlotte and I were excited about finishing INSIDE SCARS. Through the past year we had come to realize not only how much work was involved in writing a book, but also how much emotion and intensity were involved - especially for a book of this type. We had bared our souls and opened up areas of our lives that we never thought we could, or would. But mostly we were anxious to finish the book because we truly believed it would be helpful to so many people.

The conclusion of this book has been altered, however, from our original plans. About a week ago I had a dream, a dream that was so dramatically and profoundly resolving that I needed to write about it, although I'm not sure if my need to write this last chapter is for you, the reader, or for myself.

We all have different monsters that are the result of unpreventable disaster or human cruelty. Mine is incest. And although I can't undo a single part of it, I can at least reduce, if not totally change, the control I allow it to have over my life.

For the past three years I have heard many encouraging remarks from Charlotte; "Sheila, this, too, shall pass. Sheila, you can make it," and "Sheila, there is a light at the end of the tunnel." But the one that seemed to reveal the most empathy yet remained the most confusing was, "Sheila, the answers are inside of you. I can't give them to you. I can only be here and do all I can to help you find them." That statement had become discouraging. My trapped and neverending pain felt so large I couldn't imagine its resolve coming from within myself.

At the beginning of therapy I subconsciously felt and outwardly expressed the following statement, "Someone has hurt me! Won't you please make the hurt go away?!"

A little further into therapy, as I began to take some responsibility for control in my life, my subconscious statement changed slightly to, "Someone has hurt me! Won't you please help ME make the hurt go away?!" But with the insight my dream has so timely and profoundly instilled into my life, my subconscious has issued a new statement; a statement so clearly portrayed in my dream that my subconscious and conscious have joined efforts to hold on to it. It is the statement that will map out the final distance through the longest hallway of my recovery: "I am an incest survivor and the pain and devastating memories still linger inside. Please stand by me as I work to heal the scars that my incest has left within me."

I have had so many nightmares that I often struggle with wanting to go to sleep at all. Most often my nightmares are slightly rearranged reproductions of my childhood molestations. But the night of my "dream", despite enormous amounts of caffeine, I began fading fast into sleep. And as I began to dream I felt as though I consciously walked right into subconscious territory. This was to be my first "good" dream in all my twenty-eight years of life. One where, despite the incredibly frightening parts in it, I felt so much control that I tried NOT to wake up.

The dream started much like my nightmares usually do. There was an image of a life-size man. But as I looked at him he rapidly began to get larger and appeared to be coming after me. He seemed to thrive on my fear. He was everything I ever hated or feared, everything I could not stand to touch or be touched by. He was slimy, sticky, ugly, dirty, gross, smelly and dark. His face was aged with deep wrinkles. His mouth was repulsive and dirty. His eyes were wild and frightening, and they raged with terrifying threats of unmerciful pain.

My fear caused me to look away even though I was afraid to let him out of my

sight. I wanted this monster in front of me,
not over my shoulder. I began to try to dis-
solve him with the "this is not real" thought
weapon that I always carried into my sleep.
But his vivid grossness pressed for control.
I frantically looked around the room I was
in. It was barely lit and I found no door,
window or even the smallest hope of an exit.
I called out for Charlotte, longing for her
to appear from some nonexisting door, the way
she always had before. But when I finally
saw her she was standing so close to the
monster that I feared for her. She pointed
toward the monster, saying "The door, Sheila.
Go out the door." When I looked to where she
was pointing I only saw the monster. So I
tried to tell her about the monster. But she
couldn't see it. Again, she pointed toward
the monster and for a moment I didn't trust
her. But I HAD to trust her. She had always
led me out the door before.

I quickly looked back at the monster to
assure myself of his location. He had become
even bigger and uglier than before. It was
as if my fear and anxiety nurtured and fueled
him to even greater strength. I began to
panic. My fear was so great that I decided
to mutilate my body so I could be in control
of the pain. I wanted to let go of my sanity
so I could stop him from screaming into my
thoughts. Then I wanted to kill me so he
couldn't.

I looked back at his eyes, for I knew
they would give me the final thrust to my de-
mise. But when I looked straight into the pupils of his eyes I saw a flash of light. And
before my eyes could send a clear description
of what I was seeing up to my brain, I heard
myself saying out loud, "There is a door!
There really is a door!"

My eyes briefly moved away from the monster's pupils and immediately I was plagued
with fear. The door had disappeared as suddenly as it had appeared. I looked back
again. I was determined not to lose it. I

spoke directions out loud to myself; "Look
THROUGH the monster, not AT the monster. Look
INTO and BEYOND the monster. Keep the DOOR
in sight. While you have the door in sight,
RUN as fast as you can towards it!"

But my directions were halted by the
sight of the monster. He stood right in the
doorway. As I looked at him I could see that
he was standing halfway in the doorway. And
as I began to feel the threat of him again, I
realized that his size had decreased. But he
was now rapidly growing larger again. Now he
blocked the whole door; I couldn't see it.

I looked for Charlotte. Again, she was
pointing to the door. I realized then that I
would have to go straight through the eyes of
that atrocious monster to get to the door,
because if I tried to go around him he would
grow too large and consume me before I could
get there. As long as I focused only on the
door, which was deep beyond his eyes, my exit
would not be limited by the size of his eyes.

I reached for Charlotte before taking my
first step. I wanted her to go through the
eyes and out the door with me. She didn't
back away but she didn't seem to be moving
towards me either. I realized then that the
monster stood between me and the door, not
Charlotte and the door. But Charlotte would
be there, as she said she would, when I
reached the other side. I also realized that
this portion of my journey would be the hardest and scariest, for this part would be
alone. Charlotte had walked beside me for
three years, through hallway after hallway,
room after room. Now, I would have to take
all I had learned and journey this last
hallway alone. Not because Charlotte wasn't
willing to go with me, but because she could-
not. She couldn't walk through the eyes of a
monster that only I could see.

Again, I looked at the monster, and I
said "There is a door." His size didn't
increase and he didn't seem quite as strong.
I looked for Charlotte to tell her I was

ready, but my eyes caught something I hadn't seen before. There were five women, all different ages. The youngest was a child, maybe two or three years old. They seemed to be trapped and lost. They were all frozen in fear, staring straight ahead. They didn't even bat an eye when I moved in front of them. I saw the look in their eyes and their fearful expressions. Their screams from within were loud and painful and I knew they fueled the very same monster. I panicked for them and for me. I tried to get their attention but they looked beyond me to the monster. I kept telling them there was a door, but they wouldn't look at me so I could show them.

"Charlotte!" I screamed, "Please, make them stop screaming! Show them the door!" But when I looked to where Charlotte had been standing, she wasn't there. So I looked into the eyes of the monster as I said to myself, "There is a door. There is a door." This time when the door appeared, Charlotte was standing in it, arms outstretched to meet me. I would have to get myself and the five other women through the monster's eyes and to the door. I would have to keep not only the door in sight, but Charlotte as well. I would have to... My dream ended with the unwelcomed ring of the phone.

As I lay there awake, I longed for the kind of control over that monster I had experienced in the dream. I tried to engrave into my memory the image of the door I had seen. The one at the end of a scary but final hallway. The one where Charlotte stood to greet me. I whispered out loud to myself, "There is a door! There is a door!" I had found the answer that no one could give me.

XVII. EPILOGUE

Joe died two weeks before the printing of this book.

This Time I Stood Staring At You

Stunned with disbelief at what I see;
   your lifeless body in front of me.

I feel confused and my eyes start to tear
   with tears of relief instead of fear.

No more secrets to hide what you've done.
   I stand here firm, I will not run!

Later today when they bury you,
   I'll have some things to bury, too.

The guilt and shame that I have carried,
   today with your body will also be buried

I stand by your grave without guilt or
   blame.
Your life is over; mine will never be the
   same.

Yet I'll return to your grave before I'm
   through,
for I have more pain that belongs to you.

So timely and symbolic the battle I've won
   Your life has ended.
   Mine has just begun.

SUGGESTED READING

Bass, Ellen, and Thornton, Louise. I NEVER TOLD ANYONE: WRITINGS BY WOMEN SURVIVORS OF CHILD SEXUAL ABUSE. New York: Harper & Row Publishers, 1983.

Bry, Adelaide. HOW TO GET ANGRY WITHOUT FEELING GUILTY. New York: New American Library.

Butler, Sandra. CONSPIRACY OF SILENCE: THE TRAUMA OF INCEST. New York: Bantam Books, 1979.

Giaretto, Henry. TREATMENT OF CHILD SEXUAL ABUSE: A TREATMENT AND TRAINING MANUAL. Palo Alto, Ca.: Science and Behavior Books, 1982.

Gil, Eliana. OUTGROWING THE PAIN: A BOOK FOR AND ABOUT ADULTS ABUSED AS CHILDREN. San Fransisco: Launch Press, 1983.

Hanssen, Martha. SILENT SCREAM: I AM A VICTIM OF INCEST. Philadelphia: Fortress Press, 1983.

Herman, Judith Lewis. FATHER DAUGHTER INCEST. Cambridge: Harvard University Press, 1981.

Maltz, Wendy, and Holman, Beverly. INCEST AND SEXUALITY: A GUIDE TO UNDERSTANDING AND HEALING. Lexington, Mass: Lexington Books.

Russell, Diana. THE POLITICS OF RAPE: THE VICTIM'S PERSPECTIVE. New York: Stein and Day.

ORDER FORM

Pandora Press
P.O. Box 5723
Gainesville, Florida 32602
(904) 375-2739

Please send_____copy(ies)
of **INSIDE SCARS** *@8.95$ to the following:*

Name: _____

Address: _____

_____*Zip* _____

I understand that I may return any book for a full refund if not satisfied.

Florida residents   *Please add .45 cents sales tax per book*

Shipping   *$2.00 for the first book and .75 cents for each additional book*
Please allow 4 to 6 weeks for delivery.